Learn to Play Cricket

Mark Butcher and Paul Abraham

For UK order enquiries: please contact Bookpoint Ltd,
130 Milton Park, Abingdon, Oxon OX14 4SB.
Telephone: +44 (0) 1235 827720. Fax: +44 (0) 1235 400454.
Lines are open 09.00–17.00, Monday to Saturday, with a 24-h
message answering service. Details about our titles and how to
order are available at www.teachyourself.com

For USA order enquiries: please contact McGraw-Hill Customer
Services, PO Box 545, Blacklick, OH 43004-0545, USA.
Telephone: 1-800-722-4726. Fax: 1-614-755-5645.

For Canada order enquiries: please contact McGraw-Hill Ryerson
Ltd, 300 Water St, Whitby, Ontario L1N 9B6, Canada.
Telephone: 905 430 5000. Fax: 905 430 5020.

Long renowned as the authoritative source for self-guided
learning – with more than 50 million copies sold worldwide –
the Teach Yourself series includes over 500 titles in the fields of
languages, crafts, hobbies, business, computing and education.

British Library Cataloguing in Publication Data: a catalogue record
for this title is available from the British Library.

Library of Congress Catalog Card Number: on file.

First published in UK 2007 by Hodder Education, part of Hachette
UK, 338 Euston Road, London NW1 3BH.

First published in US 2007 by The McGraw-Hill Companies, Inc.

This edition published 2010.

Previously published as *Teach Yourself Cricket.*

The Teach Yourself name is a registered trade mark of
Hodder Headline.

Copyright © 2007, 2010 Mark Butcher, Paul Abraham and Gareth James

Typeset by MPS Limited, a Macmillan Company.

Printed in Great Britain for Hodder Education, an Hachette UK
Company, 338 Euston Road, London NW1 3BH, by CPI Cox &
Wyman, Reading, Berkshire RG1 8EX.

The publisher has used its best endeavours to ensure that the URLs
for external websites referred to in this book are correct and active
at the time of going to press. However, the publisher and the author
have no responsibility for the websites and can make no guarantee
that a site will remain live or that the content will remain relevant,
decent or appropriate.

Hachette UK's policy is to use papers that are natural, renewable
and recyclable products and made from wood grown in sustainable
forests. The logging and manufacturing processes are expected to
conform to the environmental regulations of the country of origin.

Impression number   10 9 8 7 6 5 4 3 2 1
Year   2014 2013 2012 2011 2010

Acknowledgements

Although numerous cricketers and cricket-lovers have had their opinions (often unwittingly) sought during the compilation of this book, the authors wish to specifically acknowledge the following for their invaluable contributions and reference materials: the James family; Ron Bush, Marc Abraham, BSc, MSc, registered dietician; Mike Brearley, author of *The Art of Captaincy*; Tom Smith, author of *New Cricket Umpiring and Scoring*; MCC, *The Spirit of the Game and the Laws of Cricket*; and Dunlop Slazenger International Ltd.

Contents

Meet the author

I hail from a family entrenched within professional cricket and therefore (thankfully) didn't stand a chance of avoiding the intricacies and the passion of this amazing sport. From before I can remember, and I'm sure like many other cricket-loving families, the discourse around the breakfast and dinner tables regularly revolved around the triumphs and tribulations of the national side, but had the additional benefit of being steeped in the fascinating first-class cricketing exploits, achievements and aspirations of my father and his brothers.

Growing up, I discovered cricket to be a tremendous test of individual character and a fantastic sport for developing a sense of team. It also has the advantage of being played during the summer months in open and often attractive spaces.

Along with the obvious physical demands of the game there are also mental challenges that engage, influence, measure and ultimately expose the courage, mental toughness and emotional state of each cricketer. I've found that the personal satisfaction experienced from overcoming these mental and physical challenges exceeds that reached in any other team sport.

Mark Butcher

Only got a minute?

A cricket match provides players, officials and spectators alike with a unique social gathering, rich in a tradition of respect and the spirit of sporting generosity that have engrained 'cricket' in our language as the byword for exemplary conduct and fair play.

Over the last few decades the most significant evolution within the sport is that cricketers are now expected to be significantly fitter and more practised than in earlier times, and cricket has reflected this improving athleticism with new and more exciting match formats, batting shots, bowling variations and fielding skills. The sport has repositioned itself as an athletic, colourful, tactically intense contest.

Cricket continues to be enjoyed by tens of millions of people around the world, with thousands of impromptu matches of differing formats taking place every day. The rules of a cricket match are easily and locally customized to take into account walls, hedges, expanses of water, roads and other inconsiderately positioned obstacles ('If you hit the ball over that wall it's six and out!'). Rules can also be relaxed to make these games more accessible to the youngest of players ('If Jasper catches the ball with one hand after one bounce, it still counts as a fair catch!').

At any age, whacking a ball over a distant wall is a memorable and satisfying experience, as is removing a batter's middle stump or taking a stunning catch. So playing in a few improvised matches is often enough for the love of cricket to worm itself under the skin. The next practical step is to start playing cricket in the more organized and regulated fixtures arranged by schools or local cricket clubs. To perform well at this level there are disciplines and skills that require specific techniques to be learned and developed.

Learn to Play Cricket is written for the improving school or club cricketer, to help develop and practise the fielding, batting, bowling and wicket keeping skills required to play cricket proficiently. Troubleshooting sections cover many common issues, and the book also examines the role of the team captain, looks at the importance of a cricketer's fitness and nutrition, and attempts to demystify the non-playing skills of umpiring and scoring.

1

The basics

In this chapter you will learn:
- *an overview of the game of cricket*
- *about the playing areas*
- *about the different formats of the game.*

The Laws

For over 250 years, all organized cricket has been regulated by a set of rules referred to as the 'Laws of Cricket' and, since 1787, the Marylebone Cricket Club (MCC) has been the sole authority for compiling these Laws. Many Laws, including the various modes of dismissal, **byes, leg byes** and what constitutes an unfair delivery can be found within the umpiring section of this book but, rather than include all the Laws of Cricket, we clarify many of the sport's regulations within the relevant skills sections.

Cricket matches are also expected to be played within what is referred to as the 'Spirit of the Game'. The Spirit of the Game is described in a preamble to the Laws and involves all cricketers showing respect to their opponents, the captains and the officials. It runs contrary to the Spirit of the Game:

- ▶ to dispute an umpire's decision by word, action or gesture
- ▶ to direct abusive language towards an opponent or umpire
- ▶ to indulge in any sharp practice such as **appealing** when knowing that the batter is not out, advancing towards an umpire in an aggressive manner when appealing or seeking to distract an opponent either verbally or by persistent clapping or making unnecessary noise under the guise of enthusiasm.

Undoubtedly the captains and the umpires set the tone for a cricket match but the Spirit of Cricket suggests that every player is expected to make positive contributions in the upholding of the sport's traditional values of good sportsmanship.

The complete and up-to-date Laws of Cricket, as well as the Spirit of the Game, can be referenced on the MCC website (www.lords.org/laws-and-spirit).

The field of play

Though not defined in the Laws, a cricket field usually has a diameter of between 120–150 metres but the size, shape and layout of cricket fields will vary from ground to ground and, in some instances, the Laws are locally modified to incorporate unusual layouts and obstacles inside the boundary. For example, for decades the Kent County ground had an enormous lime tree growing in the outfield and four runs were awarded to any batter striking the ball into it.

Around each ground a painted white line or a rope known as the boundary clearly marks the extent of the playing area.

At each end of the ground moveable sightscreens are sited just beyond this boundary. Sightscreens are white (or black when using a white cricket ball) to provide a contrast to the ball and should be positioned directly behind the bowler to assist the batter in seeing the ball as it is released from the bowler's hand.

The 'infield' is the area within approximately 30 metres of the batters and for certain formats of cricket (see section on match formats on page 5) a minimum number of fielders must be positioned within this area. When fielding restrictions are in force, the perimeter of the infield will be marked with white discs placed 30 yards (27.4 metres) from the stumps. The infield is commonly referred to as 'the circle' or 'the ring'.

In some matches there may also be a requirement for a designated number of fielders to be positioned as catchers within the 'close infield'. When this is the case two circles are marked with white discs 15 yards (13.7 metres) from the batters to indicate the perimeter of the close infield.

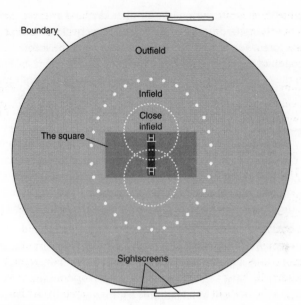

Figure 1.1 The field of play.

The 'outfield' is the area of the field between the infield and the boundary and can also be referred to as 'the deep'.

The pitch

Commonly referred to as the '**wicket**' or the '**track**', the pitch is the flat and closely mown rectangular area in the middle of the field of play on which the bowlers bowl and the batters bat. Various white lines are painted at each end of the pitch to mark out the creases. These **creases** are used by the players and umpires to assist in their judging of fair deliveries and certain modes of dismissal.

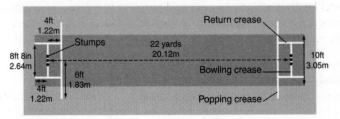

Figure 1.2 The pitch.

All pitches deteriorate during a game of cricket and after a game the pitch will be conditioned and allowed to recover for several weeks before being played on again. Most grounds therefore have a collection of eight to 12 pitches which are used in rotation. The area in the middle of the playing field encompassing this collection of pitches is known as the 'square'. Maintaining the square in a condition suitable for a fair contest is an art in itself, and therefore the pitches are often seen to be roped off between fixtures. They are usually meticulously rolled, mown and groomed by a well-schooled team of groundsmen. Upon their arrival at the ground on match day the captains, bowlers and upper-order batters habitually rush to the square to examine the results of the groundsmen's efforts in order to gather the clues from the pitch condition required to formulate their initial game plans.

Three wooden stumps are placed into the ground at either end of the pitch and wooden bails placed into grooves on top. This arrangement is collectively known as a **wicket**. Each of the three stumps is identified with the individual name of leg stump, middle stump or off stump.

The leg side and off side

The cricket field is divided in half by an imaginary line extending through both middle stumps to the boundary. It would be fairly useless to describe each of these halves as the left side or the right side because almost everyone on the field of play is facing in a different direction. For this reason the two halves are referred to as the leg side (also called the **on side**) and the off side. When the batter is in a normal set-up position, the off side is the half of the field in front of the batter and the leg side is the half behind the batter. As such, the half of the field which is considered the leg side and the off side solely depends on whether the batter is set up for right-handed or left-handed batting at the moment the bowler starts their run up to bowl a delivery.

The leg stump is the stump on the leg side, the off stump is the stump on the off side and the middle stump is, unsurprisingly, found between the leg stump and the off stump.

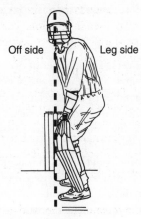

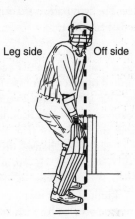

a) When the batter has a right-handed set-up

Off side   Leg side

b) When the batter has a left-handed set-up

Leg side   Off side

Figure 1.3 The leg side and off side.

Match formats

A cricket match is contested between two teams of (usually) 11 players and is divided into sessions referred to as **innings**. During each innings one team bats in pairs with the intention of accumulating as many runs as possible, while the other team takes to the field with the purpose of both restricting the scoring of runs and dismissing the opposition batters. A side is **bowled out** when ten batters have been dismissed. The remaining 'Not out' batter is not permitted to continue batting alone and the innings is closed. An innings is concluded when a side is bowled out, declares or if the allotted overs have been exhausted. During timed games, the captain of the batting side may declare their innings as concluded when they feel they have enough runs to win and be rewarded for doing so by having more time in which to bowl out the opposition side. Declarations do not occur in limited over cricket.

Each innings is divided into **overs**. An over is complete when a bowler has delivered six fair deliveries from one end of the pitch. A different bowler then starts a new over from the other end of the pitch with the umpires swapping positions (see Chapter 8). At the end of each over the fielding team will be repositioned by their captain to accommodate the change of ends and the change of bowler. The two batters do not swap their respective positions at the end of each over.

In a 'limited overs' cricket match, each team bats once and each innings is limited to usually 40 or 50 overs. The number of overs in a limited overs cricket match is designated by the league or cup competition in which the fixture is played or by the agreement of both captains prior to a friendly fixture. In limited overs cricket the side with the most runs wins and when the runs scored are equal, the side with the fewest batters dismissed wins. In the unlikely event that both sides' runs and wickets are the same then the match is deemed to be tied. A draw is not one of the potential results in limited overs cricket. Limited overs matches place a limit to the number of overs that may be bowled by each bowler and often include restrictions on how many fielders may be placed in the outfield. Fielding restrictions ensure the fielding captain cannot become over-defensive and cannot attempt to restrict the batters from scoring by placing all the side's fielders on the boundary.

The duration of a 'timed match' is based on a set period of time rather than a set number of overs. To win a timed match either the side batting first must bowl out the side batting second for fewer runs than they totalled or the side batting second must total more runs that the side batting first. Timed matches are drawn if the team batting second does not get bowled out but does not reach the total achieved by the team batting first.

Twenty20 or 'T20' is a single-innings cricket match in which each team bats for a maximum of 20 overs. This explosive format of the professional game was introduced in 2003 and immediately caught the imagination of the cricketing public. It is now seen by many as the most significant factor driving the future direction of cricket. International T20 Cricket provides the spectacle of the world's finest players in slog mode, and this has resulted in record crowds the world over. There has even been talk of T20 becoming an Olympic sport. The contrary view is that T20 may develop technically flawed players less able to contribute when competing in the more traditional versions of the game. Played at incredible speed, T20 again raises the bar for all cricketers in terms of their fitness, power, speed, agility and reaction time.

The Laws of Cricket largely apply to T20, with the following revisions:

▶ A front foot no-ball (see Umpiring) costs two runs and the next delivery is designated as a free-hit from which the batter can only be dismissed through a run out.
▶ Bowlers can bowl a maximum of four overs per innings.

The following fielding restrictions apply:

▶ No more than five fielders can be on the leg side at any time.
▶ During the first six overs a maximum of two fielders can be positioned outside the infield circle.
▶ After the first six overs, a maximum of five fielders can be positioned outside the infield circle.

If a T20 match ends with the scores tied then the tie is broken with a bowl-out. Five bowlers from each side bowl two deliveries in turn at an unguarded wicket. If the number of **wickets** is equal after the first ten deliveries per side, the bowl-out continues and the match is decided by 'sudden death', i.e. when one bowler hits and the other misses the stumps.

'Kwik cricket' is a high-speed junior version of cricket aimed mainly at encouraging children to participate. Many of the rules are adapted from cricket, but for safety and physical reasons Kwik cricket is played with a plastic bat and ball. Plastic cones mark the maximum width of a fair ball. The rules can be easily altered so that any number of children can play in the time available. The game can be made easier or more difficult to suit differing age groups by changing the physical dimensions of the pitch and field.

First-class cricket and Test matches are the formats of timed matches played by the professionals with each side batting twice and the totals for each team's innings added together. First-class matches are played over three or four days and Test matches are played over five days.

This basic outline will help those new to the sport of cricket to fathom some of the fundamentals of the game and assist in the understanding of the different formats likely to be encountered.

10 THINGS TO REMEMBER

1 The rules of cricket are referred to as the 'Laws'.

2 Cricket matches are expected to be played within the 'Spirit of the Game'.

3 The 'infield' is the area within approximately 30 metres of the batters.

4 The 'outfield' is the area of the field between the infield and the boundary.

5 The cricket pitch is the flat and closely mown rectangular area in the middle of the field of play on which the bowlers bowl and the batters bat.

6 A cricket match is contested between two teams of (usually) 11 players.

7 A cricket match is divided into sessions referred to as innings.

8 An over is complete when a bowler has delivered six fair deliveries from one end.

9 At the conclusion of each over, the fielding team will be repositioned to accommodate a change of end and a change of bowler.

10 There are differing formats of cricket, each with idiosyncratic Laws to apply.

2

Fielding

In this chapter you will learn:
- *how to approach fielding in different positions on the field of play*
- *how to catch a cricket ball*
- *skills to effectively intercept and retrieve a cricket ball*
- *the correct technique to throw a cricket ball with power and accuracy.*

The fielding side works as a unit to dismiss the opposition batters while restricting their scoring of runs and it is superior levels of energy, commitment, skill and teamwork within one side's fielding performance that often prove to be the deciding factor in a cricket match. Athletic catches, sharp interceptions and lightning throws not only take wickets and exert pressure on the batters, but also serve as valuable inspiration for the fielding side as a whole. All cricketers should therefore consider it essential to practise and sharpen their fielding skills as often as their batting or bowling.

Note

When discussing fielding we refer to all parts of the body on the same side as your throwing arm (the arm you naturally throw with) as on the 'throwing' side, i.e. the 'throwing foot' is the right foot for right-arm throwers and is the left foot for left-arm throwers. All parts of the body on the opposite side to your throwing arm are referred to as on the 'non throwing' side, i.e. the 'non throwing knee' is the left knee for right-arm throwers and is the right knee for left-arm throwers.

Fielding positions

Excluding the compulsory positions of the wicket keeper and the bowler, a fielding captain has nine fielders at his disposal and will position a number of attacking fielders within the infield with the purpose of dismissing batters by catching or running them out, and a number of defensive fielders in the outfield positioned primarily to restrict the batters scoring boundaries. According to the captain's game plan, the field may be set in an orthodox formation with an equal balance of attacking and defensive fielders, an attacking formation with more fielders placed in the infield to maximize the opportunities for taking wickets or in a defensive formation with more fielders positioned in the outfield to restrict the batters' scoring of boundaries.

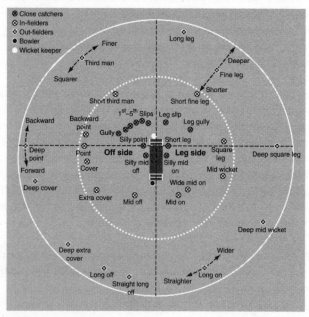

Figure 2.1 Field positions – right-handed batter.

All fielding positions have specific and often strange names but most make more sense after learning some of the following cricketing terminology.

▶ Deep – positioned further from the batter than the orthodox position, for example, deep mid-wicket.

- ▶ Deeper – move away from the batter.
- ▶ Short – positioned closer to the batter than the orthodox position, for example, short third man.
- ▶ Shorter – move towards the batter.
- ▶ Silly – positioned very close to the batter, for example, silly mid-on.
- ▶ Fine – positioned near an imaginary line extending through both middle stumps when referring to fielding positions behind the line of the batter's popping crease, for example, fine leg.
- ▶ Finer – move towards the imaginary line extending through both middle stumps when referring to fielding positions behind the line of the batter's popping crease, for example, fine leg.
- ▶ Square – positioned on or very near an imaginary line extending from the batter's popping crease, for example, square leg.
- ▶ Squarer – move towards the imaginary line extending from the batter's popping crease.
- ▶ Straight – positioned near an imaginary line extending through both middle stumps when referring to fielding positions in front of the batter's popping crease, for example, straight long off.
- ▶ Straighter – move towards the imaginary line extending through both middle stumps when referring to fielding positions in front of the batter's popping crease.
- ▶ Wide – positioned away from an imaginary line extending through both middle stumps when referring to fielding positions in front of the batter's popping crease, for example, wide mid-on.
- ▶ Wider – move away from the imaginary line extending through both middle stumps when referring to fielding positions in front of the batter's popping crease.
- ▶ Backward – behind the line of the popping crease when referring to fielding positions square of (at 90° to) the batter, for example, backward point.
- ▶ Forward – in front of the line of the popping crease when referring to fielding positions square of the batter, for example, forward short leg.

Warming up

Before fielding or practice it is essential to warm up your body in preparation for the range of movements that will be required.

A thorough warm-up prepares the body and mind for activity and reduces the likelihood of injuries. It is good practice to incorporate the specific movements you are likely to employ when fielding and therefore bending, running and turning should be an integral part of your warm-up (see Chapter 7). Once fully warmed up take a few catches and throw some balls to get your hands and eyes ready for action.

Fielding skills

When fielding in attacking or defensive positions, different techniques are employed and various skills applied. We will start with an explanation of the skills required when fielding in the attacking positions, closest to the bat, then move through infield techniques and then the defensive techniques employed in the outfield.

Close catchers

The majority of catching opportunities are offered in positions within ten metres of the batter and accordingly some of the attacking fielders are placed within the close infield in 'close', 'short' and 'silly' (very close) positions with the principal purpose of catching batters out. The ball arrives very quickly when you are positioned in positions such as slip, gully and short leg and you will need to be poised for rapid movement in any direction. It follows that a well-balanced set-up is going to be fundamental when developing proficiency in any close catching position.

SET-UP FOR CLOSE CATCHING

Try to adopt the following stance:

▶ Stand with your feet comfortably spaced, preferably shoulder width apart or slightly wider.
▶ Distribute your weight evenly on the balls of your feet.
▶ Your knees should be bent, but ensure your position is not too crouched.
▶ In readiness for a catch, your hands should be in front of your body, held together and with the fingers pointing down.

Figure 2.2 Set-up for close catching.

Insight

Because the ball can arrive very quickly and the bowler is not within the field of vision of the close fielders positioned square (at 90°) to the batter (for example, silly point, short square leg) or in front of square (for example, short mid-on/off), you should watch the batter until the ball is struck and you may be able to gather clues to the batter's intended stroke. Developing a degree of anticipation in this area can assist you to predict where the ball may go. When fielding in *all* other close positions, focus on the ball prior to it being released from the bowler's hand. Always remain fully focused on the action until the ball is considered or signalled dead (i.e. not in play).

Fielding in a close catching position will be a test of your powers of concentration. Start focusing on every delivery as the bowler starts running in to bowl so that when the ball is struck, popped up or **nicked** towards your close fielding position you are well prepared to take the catch.

Insight

Try to relax between each delivery. Create a habit of switching on your most intense focus just as the bowler turns to run in and switching off when the ball is considered or signalled dead.

Though you should be relaxed in between deliveries, it is important to keep an eye on your captain who may want to communicate a message or adjust your position in response to a batter's style, shot selection or perceived level of skill.

CATCHING

To successfully catch a fast moving cricket ball, your brain must accurately judge the pace and then correctly predict the path of the ball.

Keeping your eyes level and head steady simplifies these complex calculations and has been proved to greatly improve reaction times. For this reason try to remain perfectly still in your close fielding set-up just before and precisely as the batter strikes the ball.

To catch the ball it is crucial to keep your eyes closely focused on the ball all the way into your hands. Added to this:

▶ endeavour to let the ball come to you – don't snatch or reach forward towards the ball
▶ to soften the impact and reduce the chance of the ball bouncing out, allow your hands to 'give' as the ball is received
▶ catches arriving at and below navel level should be taken with the fingers pointing down
▶ catches arriving above navel level can be taken with the fingers pointing up
▶ remember that two hands will *always* be better than one.

Figure 2.3 Taking a catch.

Practice drill for close catching

To keep your hand–eye coordination as sharp as possible it is important for you as a cricketer to practise your close catching as regularly as possible. You can practise with a partner, a rebound net or against a wall. If practising against a wall, use a soft ball or irregularly shaped 'reaction' rubber ball designed to produce an unpredictable rebound which will demand greater concentration and quicker reactions to catch. Watch the ball at all times and pay attention to maintaining a balanced set-up. To add difficulty, move closer to your partner, net or wall.

Fielding in the infield

Attacking infielders are placed within approximately 30 metres of the batters and are considered the fielding side's strike force. Although always alert to the prospect of a catch, an infielder's most important responsibility is to challenge the batters by quickly collecting then rapidly returning the ball to the stumps. Proficient attacking fielding pressures batters by continually questioning their judgement of whether a run can safely be taken. Batters under such pressure will almost always present the fielding side with run out opportunities.

When positioned in the infield you will need to concentrate fully on each delivery and be ready to move quickly in any direction. You should bear in mind the following:

▶ start focusing on every delivery as the bowler starts running in to bowl so that when the ball is struck towards your close fielding position you are well prepared to take action
▶ as the bowler approaches his delivery stride, walk in a couple of paces towards the batter in anticipation of attacking any ball coming your way and to hasten your primary movement once the ball has been struck
▶ to facilitate moving or diving in any direction, it is important to remain balanced, to adopt a low body position and to keep your weight on the balls of your feet
▶ your head should remain steady with your eyes perfectly level
▶ in readiness for a catch or stop, your hands should be held in front of your body.

Figure 2.4 Set-up for infielders.

INTERCEPTING THE BALL IN THE INFIELD

When you are positioned in the infield your principal role is to prevent the scoring of runs by intercepting and quickly returning the ball to the stumps. When the ball is struck towards your position you will need to decide which skill is best employed for the given situation.

If the batters are considering or taking a run and you think you can prevent the single or affect a run out *and* the ball is travelling fairly slowly across the smooth surface of the infield, then the risk involved in a one-handed pick up and underarm throw is worth taking. If not, stopping the ball becomes paramount and creating a physical barrier by placing a foot or leg across the ball's path and then collecting the ball with both hands in front of this second line of defence will be the better and least risky option.

ONE-HANDED PICK UP AND UNDERARM THROW

When the ball is struck towards your fielding position and is travelling slowly across the infield a quick, short and accurate throw may be required to attempt a run out or to save a single. Under these circumstances the skill best employed by an infielder is the one-handed pick up and underarm throw. You should only employ this technique when the ball is travelling slowly across the smooth surface of the infield as any bobble will make collecting the ball in one hand almost impossible. The following points are crucial for this:

▶ as the ball comes towards you, focus your eyes on and hurry towards the ball using short steps to allow for rapid adjustments in direction
▶ get your head into line with the path of the ball
▶ in preparation to meet the ball bend your knees and adopt a low body position; the closer your eyes are to the ball, the easier it will be to collect

- ▶ keep watching the ball closely!
- ▶ pick the ball up on the outside of your throwing foot
- ▶ as you take the next step, swing back your throwing hand
- ▶ maintain your low head and body position
- ▶ select and focus on the target
- ▶ keep your weight moving forward and release the ball towards the target with a flick of the wrist
- ▶ the palm of your throwing hand should follow straight through and towards the target.

Figure 2.5 One-handed pick up.   Figure 2.6 Underarm throw.

Insight

Don't look up at the batters or the target before you have the ball in your hand as this will greatly increase the chance of a fumble.

Practice drill for one-handed pick up and underarm throw

Place three balls at varying distances from a target (for example, 5 m, 10 m and 15 m), hurry forward and using one hand pick up and throw each ball underarm at the target. You can also roll or lob a soft ball at a wall and practise the one-handed pick up and throw as the ball rebounds. Develop this drill by using both your throwing and non-throwing hand and remember that speed to the ball and an accurate return are your goals.

Collecting the ball cleanly in one hand becomes considerably more difficult when the ball has been struck towards your infield position at any speed other than slowly. Retrieving and quickly returning the ball to the stumps is always the priority of the infielder and therefore one-handed intercepts should never be attempted when it is possible to employ both hands to intercept the well-struck ball. Though it is fully understandable that every fielder will make a mistake from time to time, sloppy one-handed fielding not only creates preventable scoring opportunities for the opposition but also provides encouragement for the batters and de-motivates the fielding team as a whole. For this reason using both hands to collect the ball will always be the better technique, while at the same time positioning your foot behind your hands to act as a secondary physical barrier in case the ball is not gathered cleanly.

> **Insight**
>
> A tube of arnica cream in your kit bag can be used to treat minor bumps and reduce bruising. Rub it into the affected area during the next drinks break (read manufacturer's directions before match).

TWO-HANDED INTERCEPTS

When intercepting a ball that has been struck fairly firmly towards your infield position:

- ▶ focus your eyes on and hurry towards the ball using short steps in order to allow for rapid adjustments in your direction
- ▶ get your head into line with the path of the ball
- ▶ bend your knees and adopt a low body position to be ready to meet the ball. Remember that the closer your eyes are to the ball then the easier it will be to collect
- ▶ place your **throwing foot** behind the path of the ball. This arrangement will allow for you to most quickly adopt a good throwing position
- ▶ hold your hands together with fingers pointing down
- ▶ collect the ball with both hands directly under your eyes and in front of your throwing foot.

Figure 2.7 Two-handed intercept.

When the ball is stuck well and is speeding across the infield towards you a more significant second line of defence should be employed to ensure the ball is stopped. When intercepting a ball that is travelling rapidly towards your infield position:

▶ maintain a low body position and remember that your priority is to get your head into line with the path of the ball. You might not have time to approach the ball but do so if you can

▶ form a **long barrier** at 90° to the path of the ball by placing your non-throwing knee on the ground alongside the heel of your throwing foot. This arrangement will allow for you to most quickly adopt a good throwing position

▶ collect the ball directly under your eyes with both hands held together and your fingers pointing down.

Figure 2.8 Creating a 'long barrier'.

Diving

When fielding in the infield you may need to dive to stop the ball. When diving try to intercept the ball as late as you can and try to roll onto a shoulder upon landing to avoid both jolting the ball loose and injury.

Retrieving the ball from the infield

When the ball is struck past your infield position you will need to turn and retrieve the ball with the intention of delivering a short, sharp and accurate throw towards the stumps. In order to do this:

▶ keep your eyes focused on the ball, turn towards and chase the ball down as quickly as possible

- ▶ move to the **non-throwing side** of the ball (i.e. the left side for right-handed throwers or the right side for left-handed throwers)
- ▶ adopt a low body position and slightly overrun the ball
- ▶ pick the ball up on the outside of the throwing foot which will allow for you to most quickly adopt a good position to deliver a short accurate throw to the stumps
- ▶ turn back towards play by pivoting on your non-throwing foot and select a target.

Figure 2.9 Infield retrieve.

Insight

Always listen for guidance when you are retrieving or intercepting the ball. Are your team mates asking you to hold the ball and not risk a fast return to the stumps, or are they calling 'Bowler!' or 'Keeper!' indicating a batter in trouble and an instruction for you to throw towards one particular end?

THROWING A CRICKET BALL

Adept throwing within a team will save more runs and elicit more run outs than any other fielding skill. The only way to maximize and develop your throw's power and accuracy is to practise with a sound and smooth technique:

- ▶ grip the ball effectively, hold it across the seam with your first two fingers behind the ball and your thumb in front of the ball (see Figure 2.10)
- ▶ hold the ball with your palm facing towards the ground with the 'thumb' side of the ball towards your body
- ▶ focus your eyes on your selected target

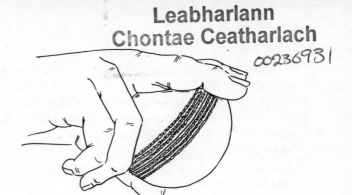

Figure 2.10 How to grip the ball.

- leading with the **non-throwing foot,** take a comfortable stride towards the target
- establish a solid base with your back foot at 90° to the line of the target
- align your non-throwing elbow with the target and draw back your throwing arm
- during the backswing, rotate your thumb upwards and open your throwing wrist (see Figure 2.11(a))
- make sure your throwing wrist is slightly outside the line of your throwing elbow
- rotate your hips first then your shoulders
- draw your non-throwing arm into your body
- hold your throwing elbow at or above shoulder level (this is vital) until the ball is released (see Figure 2.11(b))
- lead with your throwing elbow and release the ball with a flick of the wrist and your chest front on to the target (see Figure 2.11(c))
- your trailing foot (throwing foot) should remain on the ground until after the ball has been released
- follow through across your body with your throwing arm and drive through with your trailing leg (see Figure 2.11(d)).

Note

Your eyes should have been fixed on the target for the duration of the throw.

(a) Backswing

(b) Throwing action

(c) Release

(d) Follow through

Figure 2.11 Throwing a cricket ball.

Practice drill for stopping and throwing the ball

You can roll or lob a soft ball at a wall and practise all the stopping and throwing skills as the ball rebounds. Remember that speed to the ball and accurate returns are your primary goals.

Which end?

In most situations the ball should be returned quickly to the wicket keeper for it is the wicket keeper who wears the protective equipment. You should aim to throw the ball into the keeper's gloves on the full (without bouncing) and just above the bails. However, if you sense a run out opportunity at the bowler's end don't hesitate to quickly return the ball to the bowler. When throwing the ball to the bowler's end, aim to bounce the ball several metres in front of the stumps. The bowler's valuable hands are unprotected and throwing the ball 'in on the bounce' takes most of the stinging pace away from the throw, as well as ensuring the return does not rise above a comfortable catching level for the bowler.

THROWING DOWN THE STUMPS

When presented with the opportunity to run out a batter but no team mate is close enough to the stumps to collect your return you will need to aim your throw directly at the stumps. To give yourself the best chance of hitting the target keep your eyes focused on the target throughout the throw and remember it is accuracy and not power that should be your overriding consideration. Aiming at the base of the stumps will present you with the largest possible target area.

Insight

Direct hits from fielders often result in the batter being dismissed. Give yourself the best chance of success by taking the extra moment necessary to ensure you have adopted a solid and balanced throwing position.

BACKING UP IN THE FIELD

You should always remain focused on the action even if the ball has been struck towards the opposite side of the field to your position. Never assume that the wicket keeper or bowler will stop the ball when it is returned or that a ball struck firmly towards a team mate will be collected cleanly. Whenever possible and in order to provide back-up for the return, move quickly to a position ten to 15 metres behind any team mate attempting to collect the ball. By backing up well, all fielders, but particularly fielders in the infield, can protect their team against over-throws (extra runs) scored from misfields, bad bounces or wild returns.

It is also important that an infielder gets into position and is prepared to receive any return to the stumps when either the wicket keeper or the bowler has abandoned their usual position to retrieve the ball.

When you are the fielder best positioned to fulfil this role, move quickly behind the stumps (relative to the ball) holding both hands together and over the bails. Focus on the return throw from the fielder and closely watch the ball right into your hands. Do not look at the batters or shift your attention towards the stumps before you have the ball in your hands. Once you have safety collected the return throw you may need to 'break the wicket' to run out any batter who has not made the necessary ground to get behind the line of the popping crease. Breaking the wicket involves dislodging at least one bail from the stumps with either the ball or the hand(s) holding the ball. If both bails have already been dislodged (for example, in a prior stumping or run out attempt) and if you have time you may replace one or both bails. If on the other hand there is no time to replace a bail, then you can break the wicket by pulling a stump from the ground with the hand or hands holding the ball.

CATCHING IN THE INFIELD

Though the principal role of the infielder is to intercept and quickly return the ball to the stumps, those positioned in the infield must also be alert to opportunities to catch batters out. When the ball is struck in the air towards your infield position:

- ▶ focus your eyes on the ball and move quickly to get your head into line with the ball's path
- ▶ keep your head as steady as you can and make sure your eyes remain level
- ▶ hold your hands together and in front of your body. Your fingers should be spread and pointing down for catches arriving at navel level and below. Your fingers can be pointing up for higher catches
- ▶ keep watching the ball closely until it is right in your hands
- ▶ attempt to catch the ball with both hands held together
- ▶ let your hands give as the ball is received to soften the impact and reduce the chance of the ball bouncing out.

When taking high catches you must clearly call to your team mates to identify yourself as the catcher. Use your name, for example, 'Jenson's!' as two or three fielders calling 'Mine!' can lead to misunderstandings. Clear calling avoids nasty collisions between converging fielders. If two or more fielders call for the same ball it then becomes the captain's responsibility to identify which fielder holds the best position to make the catch and to immediately and clearly call that fielder's name. The non-catching fielder or fielders must then immediately pull out of their attempt and look to avoid the nominated catching fielder whose entire focus should remain on the ball.

Fielding in the outfield

Defensive fielders are positioned in the outfield and on the boundary with the responsibility of intercepting or retrieving any ball struck beyond the infielders. The ball is collected then returned quickly to the stumps to restrict the batters' scoring of twos, threes and boundary fours. All defensive fielders should concentrate on the action from when the bowler starts his run-up and be watching the ball from the moment it is released from the bowler's hand. When you are placed in a defensive field position also remember to keep a close eye on your captain in between deliveries. A good skipper often prefers to use subtle hand movements when indicating adjustments to their fielding positions rather than draw the batters' attention to any changes in strategy.

Insight

When positioned 'on the boundary' (unless otherwise instructed by your captain) be no more than five metres from the boundary when the ball is struck. Don't be tempted to creep any closer to the action as this will limit the length of boundary you can properly protect and also make catching just inside the boundary significantly more difficult as you will need to turn and attempt the catch with the ball arriving over your shoulder.

As the bowler approaches his delivery stride, 'walk in' towards the batter in anticipation of the ball coming your way and to hasten your primary movement once the ball has been struck. You must be prepared to sprint in any direction so it is important to remain relaxed, balanced, to keep your weight moving forward and to be on the balls of your feet. Your head should be steady with your eyes perfectly level. Hold both hands in front of your body in readiness to intercept the ball.

INTERCEPTING THE BALL IN THE OUTFIELD

An outfield is never perfectly smooth and a cricket ball travelling across this area has every chance of bobbling or taking an unexpected turn. When the ball is travelling across the outfield towards your outfield position, stopping the ball and preventing a boundary four is paramount, so using both of your hands to collect the ball while forming a physical barrier behind the ball to act as a second line of defence guarding against any misfield will always be the best and safest technique to employ. The speed the ball is travelling and the condition of the outfield will dictate which barrier will be better employed.

When the ball has been struck well and is travelling rapidly across the outfield or the outfield is particularly uneven and the ball is not following a predictable path, focus on the ball as soon as it has been struck and hurry into line with its path. Adopt a low body position and in case the ball is not gathered cleanly, form a 'long barrier' at 90° to the path of the ball by placing your non-throwing knee on the ground alongside the heel of the throwing foot (see Intercepting the ball in the infield on page 16). Collect the ball directly under your eyes with both hands held together. Your fingers should be pointing down and comfortably spread.

A ball moving more slowly across a relatively even outfield should be intercepted with both hands in front of your throwing foot.

RETRIEVING THE BALL IN THE OUTFIELD

When the ball is struck past your position in the outfield you will need to turn and retrieve the ball with the intention of delivering a long throw back towards the stumps. Retrieving the ball with the intention of delivering a long throw requires a different technique than when a shorter throw is required as a step is taken towards the target to develop extra momentum and power in the throwing action. Make sure you:

- ▶ keep your eyes fixed on the ball, turn towards it and chase the ball down
- ▶ move to the **non-throwing side** of the ball (left side for right-handed throwers or right side for left-handed throwers)
- ▶ adopt a low body position and slightly overrun the ball
- ▶ pick the ball up **inside the non-throwing foot,** which will allow you to quickly adopt a good position to deliver a long throw towards the stumps
- ▶ turn back towards play using the throwing foot as a pivot and select a target.

Figure 2.12 Retrieving the ball in the outfield.

THE SLIDE

Professional cricketers are routinely seen sliding to the ground to collect the ball. This technique saves time as the momentum of the slide allows the pick up, stand up and throw to be completed within one action. The slide can be employed when either retrieving or intercepting the ball. When sliding:

▶ fix your eyes on the ball and run to the **non-throwing side** of the ball (i.e. the right side of the ball for a right-handed thrower or the left side for a left-handed thrower)
▶ once you are close enough to the ball, slide feet first, just beyond the ball and onto your non-throwing hip and leg
▶ collect the ball with your throwing hand
▶ straighten the throwing leg and get upright by using the momentum of the slide to place weight on your straightened throwing leg in combination with pushing yourself up with your non-throwing arm.

Figure 2.13 The slide.

THROWING FROM THE OUTFIELD

When throwing from the deep it is most important to focus on the target (usually the wicket keeper's gloves) and to make sure you adopt a solid and balanced throwing position. You should aim the throw to arrive just above the stumps either without bouncing or after one bounce to allow for a comfortable, stump high take. Improving and practising your throwing technique will help to develop power and accuracy (see page 20).

Your primary purpose as an outfielder is to return the ball to the stumps quickly enough to restrict the batters when they are considering another run. Under no circumstances retain the ball in the outfield as in most cases the batters will be able to steal the extra run you were positioned to defend against.

Incorporating a 'crow hop' within your throwing action will generate extra momentum towards the target and therefore will allow you to throw a ball further and with more power. After you have collected the ball:

- ▶ select and focus on a target
- ▶ adopt a side-on position to the target
- ▶ pass your throwing foot closely behind your non-throwing foot in order to create forward momentum and to maintain your side-on position
- ▶ establish a solid base and throw the ball towards the target.

Figure 2.14 The crow hop.

THE RELAY THROW

Adopted from cricket's distant cousin, American baseball, the relay throw is the quickest method to return a ball from long boundaries when the retrieving outfielder is too distant to be able to throw the ball directly to the stumps. The relay throw can also be employed as an aggressive method of attempting a run out.

When employing a relay throw, the nearest infielder hurries to get aligned between the retrieving outfielder and the wicket keeper. When moving into this relay position it is vital for the infielder to present a clear target for the outfielder's throw and also to remain alert to the positions of the batters. The infielder should also be calling and indicating to the outfielder that a relay throw is on. After retrieving the ball the outfielder makes a strong and accurate throw to the infielder's mid-section and it is then the infielder's responsibility to quickly pivot and relay the throw towards the stumps.

CATCHING IN THE OUTFIELD

Outfielders can be required to take high catches which, though they may appear so to the uninitiated, are rarely simple. The ball may be swirling in the wind, coming out of the sun, trees or other such distracting influence. The fielder may also need to cover significant ground. Even without these external complications, the time a soaring cricket ball stays airborne can feel like an eternity and provide the necessary space for numerous worries to manifest in the apprehensive fielder's head. Confidence is fundamental to consistently taking skied catches and it is a solid practised technique that provides our confidence. The two techniques employed by cricketers for taking high catches are the 'orthodox' and the 'reverse' techniques.

Orthodox
With this technique:

- ▶ keep your head steady, focus on the ball and hurry to get positioned directly under the dropping ball
- ▶ establish a solid and balanced base with your knees slightly bent
- ▶ raise both hands to or above eye level

▶ hold both hands together with your little fingers touching and spread your fingers
▶ keep watching the ball right into your hands
▶ catch the ball at or just below eye level
▶ close your hands around the ball and collect the ball into your chest to soften the impact and lessen the chance of the ball bouncing out.

      (a) Orthodox set-up   (b) Orthodox catch

Figure 2.15 The orthodox technique.

Reverse

With this technique:

▶ keep your head steady, focus on the ball and hurry to get into a position directly under the ball
▶ establish a solid and balanced base with your knees slightly bent
▶ raise both your hands above eye level
▶ with your thumbs touching, hold both hands together and spread your fingers
▶ keep watching the ball right into your hands
▶ catch the ball above eye level
▶ close your hands around the ball and collect the ball towards either shoulder to soften the impact and lessen the chance of the ball bouncing out.

(a) Reverse set-up   (b) Reverse catch

Figure 2.16 The reverse technique.

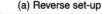

Practice drill for catching in the outfield

Practise with a partner or throw a cricket or tennis ball high and catch it. Remember that it is critical to your success to adopt a solid and balanced body position under the ball and to watch the ball closely right into your hands.

Cricket is a team game and whether or not you have done well with the bat or the ball you should always aspire to excel as a fielder and to make fielding an important area of your contribution to the team. Commitment and confidence in your own abilities will be the key components to your success as an all-round fielder. Fielding drills should therefore be practised regularly enough to ensure that you maintain the personal level of confidence where you **expect** to safely intercept, retrieve and catch every ball that comes your way.

Troubleshooting

Here are some common fielding problems along with some possible solutions.

I'M DROPPING TOO MANY CATCHES

This is a common problem but dropping a catch or two in a match can be a most demoralizing experience and happens to all cricketers from time to time. The most crucial issue here is that you should have practised taking catches to the level where you have the confidence in your ability to hang onto the ball when it arrives.

If you are dropping too many catches then there is a good chance that it is a lack of confidence that is creating a flaw in your catching technique.

Solution: Only regular practice can rectify a lack of confidence so take a soft ball outside and practise. Develop your confidence by introducing a cricket ball to your practice.

Another reason is that you are taking your eyes off the ball momentarily before it arrives.

Solution: Ensure that you closely watch the ball all the way from the bat until it is safely in your hands.

It may be that you have not adopted a steady head and/or body position behind or under the ball.

Solution: Don't panic! When the ball is hit in the air towards your fielding position get a good sight of the ball then get into line with the ball as quickly and as smoothly as possible. Try to remain relaxed and keep your eyes level and maintain a steady head position to give yourself the best chance of successfully judging the catch. Create a balanced and stable base to your body position by slightly bending your knees and distributing your weight evenly on the balls of your feet.

It might also be the case that your hands are not 'giving' with the catch. Not absorbing some of the power of the ball will encourage the ball to bounce from and out of your hands. This problem is commonly referred to as 'hard hands'.

Solution: (a) Infielder – as the ball arrives ensure your hands are held together and in front of your body and then draw them into your body as the catch is taken. (b) Outfielder – as the ball arrives ensure your hands are held together at or above eye level and then draw them into a shoulder as the catch is taken. In either situation your hands should never snatch at or move forward towards the ball.

I HAVE A WEAK THROW OR MY SHOULDER ACHES WHEN I THROW

A possible reason for a weak throw is that you are not establishing a solid base or a good enough throwing position.

Solution: Ensure you are throwing with both your feet placed on the ground and that you are taking a comfortable but decent stride towards the target.

Another reason could be that you are not following through.

Solution: As the ball is released, ensure your weight is moving forwards by aggressively driving your throwing leg through and towards the target.

A possible reason for a sore shoulder is that your throwing elbow has fallen below shoulder level.

Solution: Practise throwing with the correct technique by ensuring you maintain your throwing elbow at or above shoulder level throughout the throwing action.

MY THROW IS CONSISTENTLY INACCURATE

A possible reason for an inaccurate throw is that your grip is incorrect and the ball is swinging away from your target.

Solution: Ensure your grip on the ball is around the seam.

Another reason could be that your non-throwing elbow is not aligned with the target.

Solution: Create the habit of looking at the target along the inside of your non-throwing elbow.

Alternatively, your body position might not be side-on to the target.

Solution: Ensure that your throwing foot is positioned at 90° to the target.

I STRUGGLE TO MAINTAIN CONCENTRATION WHILE FIELDING

Fielding for long periods is mentally arduous but your concentration must be maintained. Lapses in concentration will always make fielders appear to have a lack of appreciation of the importance of team fielding. This will encourage the batters, will act to frustrate the bowlers and can de-motivate the fielding side as a whole.

One reason for a lapse in concentration is that you are trying to concentrate for extended periods, finding this impossible to maintain and then becoming mentally tired.

Solution: Develop and implement a process whereby you can switch on and switch off your focus to certain cues within the game, for example, switch on your focus as the bowler starts his run up and then consciously relax once the ball is signalled or considered dead.

10 THINGS TO REMEMBER

1 The fielding side's role is to work as a unit in order to dismiss the opposition batters while restricting the scoring of runs.

2 Cricketers should practise their fielding skills as often as their batting or bowling.

3 To avoid injury, it is essential to warm up your body in preparation for the range of movements that will be required when fielding or practising fielding.

4 Attacking fielders are positioned within the infield, with the primary purpose of dismissing batters by catching or running them out.

5 Defensive fielders are positioned in the outfield primarily to restrict the batters scoring boundaries.

6 Keep an eye on your captain in between deliveries.

7 As the bowler approaches his delivery stride, walk in towards the batter in anticipation of attacking any ball coming your way.

8 Keeping your head steady and your eyes level and fixed on the ball is the simplest way to improve most of your fielding skills.

9 Two hands will always be better than one.

10 When fielding, the ball should normally be immediately returned to the wicket keeper.

3

Batting

In this chapter you will learn:
- *how to approach your innings as an individual and as a team player*
- *the full range of batting strokes*
- *techniques for batting against various bowling styles*
- *about running between the wickets.*

Every cricketer is expected to contribute to their team's batting effort irrespective of their position in the batting order and, put simply, the expected contribution of each batter during the normal course of play is to score runs as quickly as possible without getting dismissed. Of course even the best batters holding the most disciplined of intentions can and will get out and that is the reason why in the sport of cricket, everyone gets to bat. There is also the added complication that various situations within a game will often dictate that it becomes necessary for the batter to either play defensively in order to protect wickets or to strike out aggressively in an attempt to improve the team's scoring of runs.

Batting as a team – partnerships

Prior to each innings it is the captain's responsibility to decide the team's batting order. The captain may change this batting order at any point during the innings either when different game situations are encountered or if it is considered that a change of strategy is required.

The number one and two batters open the team's innings and are referred to as the 'opening batters' or '**openers**'. Numbers three and four complete what is referred to as the 'upper order'. The 'middle order' comprises the number five, six and seven batters. The 'lower order' usually consists of a team's bowlers. The team's lower order is commonly referred to as 'the tail' consisting of the **'tail-enders'**.

An important quality to a side's successful batting effort is that they perform well within these partnerships. Productive partnerships achieve more than just adding runs to the total; productive batting partnerships also serve to frustrate and drain energy from the fielding side by making their best efforts appear fruitless.

THE UPPER ORDER

The opening batters and the upper order will almost certainly be facing a new ball. This ball is hard, polished and probably in the hands of the opposition's best exponents of swing and seam bowling. These **'strike' bowlers** will be at their freshest and initially the fielding positions will be set aggressively with every likelihood of several attacking fielders being positioned in close catching positions (such as one or two slip fielders and a gully) as well as a ring of infielders positioned to restrict the batters scoring easy singles from non-attacking strokes. Upper order batting **partnerships** are charged with the responsibility of either patiently seeing off these aggressive opening bowling **spells** or getting the innings off to a flying start by taking the attack back to these bowlers in an attempt to disrupt the fielding side's game plan and ensure that the attacking fielders are quickly repositioned more defensively. Either way successful upper order batting requires a sound batting technique.

THE MIDDLE ORDER

As the innings develops it becomes the middle order partnerships' role to maintain or even progress the scoring momentum. Therefore middle order batters must possess the ability to score fluently from both pace and spin bowling. The middle order also needs to react defensively or aggressively in response to any unplanned situation the batting side find themselves in. To fill these requirements middle order batters need to be more versatile and free-scoring than the upper order.

THE LOWER ORDER

When only one specialist batter remains, the senior batter's mission becomes one of shepherding the lower order while either attempting to score as many runs as possible or simply to survive throughout the remaining overs in an attempt to avoid defeat. This is achieved by exposing the 'tail-enders' to as little bowling as possible by declining singles early in each over, scoring in twos, fours and sixes and then pinching a single run during the final couple of deliveries of each over. This tactic is referred to as 'farming the strike'. Productive lower order partnerships add valuable runs and frustrate the fielding side who had hoped a few quick wickets would end the innings.

Preparing to bat

Intelligent batting starts with studied and continued awareness so, unless opening the batting, it is advisable to watch your teammates develop the innings. Watching the game unfold can provide you with much of the information you will need to plan your own innings. When preparing to bat, sit outside the pavilion in order to let your eyes become better accustomed to the available light. Analyse and consider how the conditions may affect your batting strategy. Are the conditions producing unusual bounce, swing or is the pitch particularly conducive to spin? Also carefully assess the opposition and then explore possible strategies to counter the strengths and exploit the weaknesses of the opposition bowlers, fielders and tactics. Identify which shots will carry the most and least risk given these variables and visualize yourself batting accordingly. A positive mental attitude will also be required to win the duel with the bowlers. Professional cricketers are taught to spend the time immediately before batting imagining themselves in the middle, batting successfully and striking the ball with a full range of the most appropriate batting strokes.

Insight

Before you bat (or early in your innings if you are opening the innings) observe which throwing hand the infielders are using and identify which fielders are particularly proficient and which are weak. This will help you to establish where taking a run will be most risky and also where easy extra runs may be scored.

Warming up and stretching is an equally important aspect of a batter's preparation (see Chapter 7) and as a flurry of wickets can mean a batter is required at the crease with little notice it becomes important for batters to remain warm and loose throughout their team's batting innings. A proper warm-up raises mental awareness, improves coordination, improves the elasticity and contractibility of muscles and increases the efficiency of the respiratory and cardiovascular systems.

In summary, proper physical and mental preparation makes for easier and more confident batting at the beginning of an innings when batters are at their most vulnerable.

TAKING GUARD

Once at the wicket it is important to know where your head and feet are positioned relative to the stumps behind you. Therefore, before you face your first delivery, hold your bat upright on the popping crease and check its position with the umpire standing at the bowler's end of the pitch by stating the stump or stumps you wish your bat to be placed directly in front of and adjusting the bat's position accordingly. This procedure of selecting a default batting position is called taking guard. Taking guard helps you to accurately judge whether each delivery will hit or miss the stumps so you can adequately defend your wicket and employ the most appropriate batting stroke. The most commonly requested guards are either 'one leg' (leg stump), 'two legs' (between middle and leg stump) or 'middle stump'. The umpire will indicate whether you need to move your bat towards or away from you in order for the bat to be in perfect alignment with your requested guard.

Your guard is entirely a matter of personal preference and as experience is gained all cricketers settle upon the guard that best suits their own style of play. Batters who are strong on the leg side will usually take a middle stump guard in order to play more shots

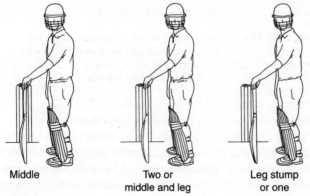

| Middle | Two or middle and leg | Leg stump or one |

Figure 3.1 Taking guard.

towards the leg side. Strong drivers of the ball often adopt a more leg side guard to create the room to strike more deliveries through the covers.

If you are not sure which guard to adopt, two legs (middle and leg stump) is a good place to take guard as your head will be positioned directly in line with middle stump when you set up correctly.

Once the umpire has confirmed your guard, mark the pitch on or around the line of the popping crease with either your studs, the toe of the bat or a bail thus ensuring that throughout your innings you know exactly where you are positioned in relation to the stumps. You can and should adjust, re-check and re-mark your guard as often as you think necessary.

A batter's guard will routinely be adjusted against a bowler who changes the angle of his deliveries. A right-arm bowler who changes his delivery from 'over the wicket' (i.e. runs in and bowls from the left side of the umpire) to round the wicket' (i.e. runs in and bowls from the right side of the umpire) will often find the batter requests a more leg side guard to accommodate the change in angle. This would equally be the case when a right-handed batter faces a left-arm bowler bowling over the wicket (i.e. runs in and bowls from the right side of the umpire). The wider angle of delivery a left-arm bowler produces bowling round the wicket (i.e. runs in and bowls from the left side of the umpire) may encourage the batter to request a guard further towards the off stump. These adjustments in guard will all be made according to the angle of the delivery and with the intention of producing a consistent set-up position for the batter to assist in his judgement of his position relative to the stumps.

SURVEYING THE FIELD

Excluding the bowler and wicket keeper, the fielding captain has only nine fielders available to restrict your scoring. Obviously you will score most runs in the gaps between these fielders so when surveying the field identify the gaps where your easiest runs will be scored. Attacking fielders are also placed to catch you out, so be mindful of which stroke or strokes carry the most risk given the set field. An example of this is if two or three slips and a gully are positioned behind you, then playing shots away from the body, for example, front foot drives to deliveries pitched on a good **length** or to deliveries directed on a line outside the off-stump, carries a significantly greater degree of risk of an edged delivery being caught than if those positions are vacant. As the field positions change ensure your batting game plan changes accordingly. Remember that the fielding captain will not inform the batter of any change in field position, so continue surveying the field throughout your innings.

PLAYING YOURSELF IN

Whether you are sent in to open the batting or to score rapid runs in the final overs, it pays to 'play yourself in'. In normal batting situations three to four overs of quiet and watchful batting is considered a normal playing in period, but do use your own common sense and if there are only a few deliveries remaining in the innings you really only have one delivery to have a look. The primary objective during playing yourself in is to watch the ball closely. The process of playing yourself in is intended to achieve the following:

▶ so your eyes can become better accustomed to watching a moving ball in the light available
▶ to allow your hand and eye coordination to start functioning smoothly
▶ so you become better accustomed to the conditions, the pace, bounce and any lateral movement of the bowling.

The batting grip

A correct batting grip allows your hands and wrists to work together as a single pivot point and is therefore fundamental to successfully developing and executing the full range of batting strokes.

For a right-handed batter, the left hand should be at the top of the bat handle and vice versa for a left-handed batter. All other grip principles are the same for right- and left-handed batters.

▶ Position your hands together towards the top of the bat handle.
▶ The 'V's formed by the thumb and first finger of each hand should line up centrally between the back **edge** (splice) and leading edge of the bat.

▶ The bat should be gripped firmly but your arms and shoulders should remain relaxed.

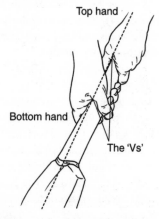

Top hand

Bottom hand

The 'Vs'

Figure 3.2 The grip of a right-handed batter.

▶ The 'top hand' controls most shots and the 'bottom hand' provides the guidance but also supplies extra power when required.
▶ Check that your top hand is correctly aligned when the knuckle of the first finger lines up with the outside edge of the bat.

Insight

To ensure your top hand controls your shots, hold the bat relatively loosely with your bottom hand compared to the top hand grip.

The batting stance

A batter needs to be able to move according to each delivery and therefore a balanced set-up is a key element of batting and is evident within any good stance. Any batter whose head leans over to one side or whose weight is placed too solidly on either leg will almost certainly restrict their ability to execute fluently the full complement of cricket shots.

Your feet should be placed wide enough to ensure comfort and perfect balance. Orthodox coaching methods suggest feet should be shoulder width apart but many great players have found success with a wider than normal stance while others have flourished while standing with their feet closer together.

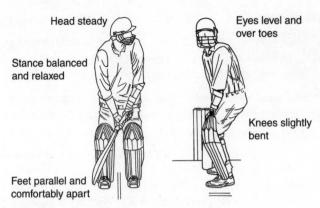

Head steady

Stance balanced
and relaxed

Eyes level and
over toes

Knees slightly
bent

Feet parallel and
comfortably apart

Figure 3.3 Batting stance.

Stand sideways on to the bowler with both feet parallel to the crease. Usually one foot should be placed either side of the popping crease so you don't run the risk of knocking over your own stumps when playing a stroke and so you remain protected against a stumping by keeping a foot behind the line of the popping crease. Your weight should be evenly distributed on the balls of your feet and your knees slightly bent. Ensure your head remains steady and level and face the bowler with your eyes directly over your toes.

Insight

To strike a moving cricket ball the batter's brain must analyse an array of visual information within a split second. Holding the head steady and keeping the eyes perfectly level aids this complex task and has been proved to significantly quicken a batter's reactions.

Practice drill

1 Find a long mirror or window where you can see your full reflection.
2 Make sure you have plenty of room in all directions, including above you!
3 Place a box or set of stumps behind you and take up your batting stance facing your reflection.
4 Check your grip (especially your Vs and that your bottom hand and arms are relaxed).
5 Check your stance (especially the position of your feet, head and eyes). Your goal is to find a relaxed and balanced stance while ensuring your eyes remain level and directly over your toes.

Watch the ball!

Remember – Without first and foremost closely watching the ball from the bowler's hand until the moment it strikes the bat face, every other batting skill you can employ is worthless!

With head steady, eyes level and early focus, the brain can more quickly track the ball's path and speed and as a result you will get into the best position more quickly to play a shot.

Set yourself up in a comfortable stance as the bowler turns to bowl and fix your eyes on the ball in hand. Assess the grip the bowler has on the ball. This technique will ensure you are watching the ball closely enough and help develop the skill of '**picking**' a bowler's variations by noticing the small changes in the bowler's grip or wrist position. To help develop this skill more quickly, read the bowling sections to learn how different styles of bowler, trying to do different things with a ball, employ different grips to achieve their ambitions.

Insight

When attempting to strike a cricket ball it is important to realize that the ball will rebound with significantly more power if struck with the heaviest section of the bat found within the lower half of the bat face. We refer to this sweet spot as the 'middle' of the bat, but it is actually situated lower down the bat face than the geometric middle. Dropping a cricket ball on different areas of your bat face will quickly identify this sweet spot as the ball will bounce significantly higher from the bat's 'middle'.

A common problem when batting is taking the eyes off the ball before impact. This critical error is often seen within ugly slogs, with the embarrassing consequence of the batter missing the ball entirely. It is very important to practise your ball watching skills regularly.

Practice drill

Adopt a side on batting stance to a wall and rebound a tennis or golf ball off the wall while gripping a cricket stump (as a bat) in your top hand. Attempt to strike the ball on the rebound using properly executed cricket shots. You will quickly learn that to even touch the ball regularly you must first and foremost carefully 'watch the ball'. Narrow 'coaching bats' are available and are ideal for this drill.

As your bottom hand is engaged late in the action, this drill also very helpfully encourages a dominant top hand within the batting strokes.

This drill was adopted and its virtues celebrated by Sir Don Bradman, the Australian batsman with the highest batting average in Test match history.

Understanding length

The length of a delivery refers to the distance the ball bounces (pitches) in front of the batter and influences which batting strokes can be employed. The length of a delivery varies depending on a batter's height, the pace of the bowling and the pitch conditions. In simple terms any delivery described as 'short' will pitch (bounce) some distance in front of the batter and the ball will rise to or above the waist level of the batter and encourage the batter to employ a back foot stroke described later in this section. In contrast, deliveries referred to as 'full' or on the 'half volley' will pitch much closer to the batter, will not have time to rise above the batter's knee level, will draw the batter forward and encourage the front foot shots described later in this section. A delivery of 'good' length refers to a delivery that pitches in between a short and full-length delivery, is just beyond the reach of the batter and at a length where 'front foot or back foot?' becomes quite a tricky judgement. The decision is more difficult because at the point of impact, the ball has risen above the level at which it can be comfortably 'driven' with the bat's middle but is still below the level that a back foot shot becomes the obvious option. Scoring from good length bowling is problematic and batting successfully against bowlers who consistently pitch deliveries on a good length requires patience, shot discipline, some strategy and a sound technique.

A **yorker** length delivery is pitched on or around the popping crease and is aimed to sneak under the bat.

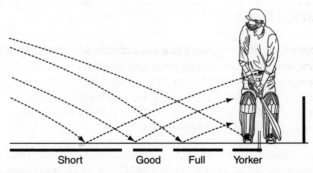

Figure 3.4 Different lengths of delivery.

Getting into line

The line of a delivery describes how far to the leg side or the off side the ball is directed. The line of a delivery controls the width within which you have to operate as a batter and also influences which batting strokes can be correctly employed. Getting your eyes into line with a delivery is a prerequisite to being in a good position to play a shot. Getting into line requires a backswing of the bat with a positive step forward or backward and towards the line of the delivery. In order to maintain good balance this backswing and step should be performed together in one smooth action.

BACKSWING AND STEP

The principal objectives of the backswing and step are:

▶ to move your eyes into line with the delivery
▶ to attain a wider and therefore more stable base to your stance
▶ to raise the bat into a position from which your selected shot can be effectively executed
▶ to ensure your weight is forward as you strike the ball.

During the backswing and step it is important to keep your head steady with your eyes held perfectly level and focused on the ball. Use your shoulders, arms and bat to work together as one component during the backswing and ensure your back elbow travels straight back and remains clear of your body. At the top of the backswing your hands should be close to your back hip with the toe of the bat held at approximately shoulder level. The bat should be pointing towards the position of first slip and the bat face should be open.

PLAYING FORWARD (FRONT FOOT STROKES)

When a delivery is pitched on a full length you should play forward and strike the ball just after it has pitched by taking a step forward towards the pitch of the ball. Make sure that:

▶ while maintaining focus on the ball, you move your head smoothly into line with the delivery
▶ following your head's lead, your front shoulder dips forward and both elbows bend as the bat is swung backwards
▶ following your head's lead, you take a comfortable but positive stride towards the line of the delivery

▶ you keep your bottom hand grip relaxed and use your top hand to control the bat throughout the backswing.

Figure 3.5 Backswing and step forward.

PLAYING BACK (BACK FOOT STROKES)

When a delivery is pitched on a short length you should take a step back in the crease and strike the ball after it has risen to or above waist level. To do this:

▶ while maintaining focus on the ball, move your head smoothly into line with the delivery
▶ following your head's lead, make sure your front shoulder dips forward and both elbows bend as the bat is swung backwards
▶ your back foot steps deeply back into the crease and across the stumps into the line of the delivery
▶ keep your bottom hand grip relaxed and use your top hand to control the bat throughout the backswing.

Figure 3.6 Backswing and step back.

Shot selection

After committing to the front foot or back foot step you will then need to judge which deliveries to attack, which to defend and which to leave alone. Your shot selection is dependent on variables such as how long you've been batting, the position of the fielders, the pitch condition, the line, length and speed of the delivery, your team's required run rate or the state of the game. However, you can use Figure 3.7 to give you a guide to which shots are considered to be the most orthodox given the line and the length of the delivery.

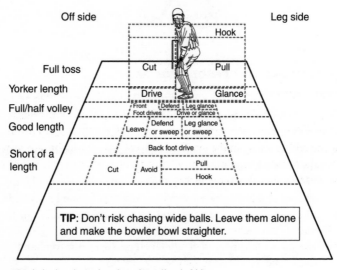

Figure 3.7 Orthodox shot selection depending on line and length of delivery.

Insight

Don't risk chasing wide balls. Leave them alone and make the bowler bowl straighter.

Batting against pace bowling

Almost all teams take to the field with three or four medium or fast paced bowlers so it follows that a sound technique against pace bowling is a prerequisite for any successful batting career. The long run up and a grip with fingers positioned behind the ball will be your first clues that a bowler may be attempting to swing or seam the ball at pace.

'Seam bowlers' bowl at a medium to fast pace – 65–95 mph (105–150 kph) – and try to pitch the ball's seam on a good length to achieve a sharp deviation in the delivery. The ball may seam into or away from the batter. Seam bowlers want the batter to miss or edge the ball by prematurely committing to a stroke down the incorrect line (see Chapter 4).

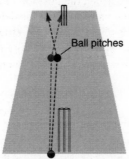

Figure 3.8 Delivery of a seam bowler.

'Swing bowlers' also bowl at medium to fast pace and will endeavour to pitch their deliveries full in length to allow the maximum distance for the ball to swing in the air. The delivery may swing into or away from the batter. Swing bowlers also want the batter to prematurely commit to a shot down the wrong line.

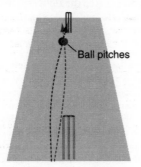

Figure 3.9 Delivery of a swing bowler.

As a batter it is important to rise to the challenge of pace bowling and very satisfying to be seen to relish the test with skill and courage. When batting against pace bowling it can be helpful to remember that run scoring is potentially an easier task as the ball need not be struck powerfully to still have every chance of racing away to the boundary. You also have the knowledge that the wicket keeper is likely to be standing back from the stumps which allows you to move forward towards the pitch of the deliveries without the prospect of being stumped.

To successfully play pace bowling:

▶ play yourself in and get used to the pace and bounce of the bowling
▶ watch the bowler's hand carefully for any alterations in the grip or wrist position that would indicate some variation in the delivery (see Chapter 4)
▶ be alert to the possibility that the bowler is bowling from a wider position than usual in an attempt to deceive you with a change in the line of attack
▶ watch the ball along the entire path of the delivery
▶ do not commit yourself too early to a line or a shot
▶ avoid playing at wide deliveries because it is difficult to get in line with the wider delivery in time to execute an appropriate batting stroke and therefore significantly increases the chance of mistiming the shot
▶ when the ball is seaming or swinging avoid employing attacking strokes to good length deliveries as the lateral movement of the ball could easily result in you edging the ball and the loss of your wicket. Even if you survive the delivery, an imprudent swing significantly boosts a bowler's confidence.

Insight

Pace deliveries of a good line and length can be difficult to score from. When the wicket keeper is standing back from the stumps, don't be afraid to take guard as far as a yard outside the popping crease in order to disrupt the rhythm of the pace bowler who will need to adjust the length of the delivery to avoid bowling half volleys. This strategy also reduces the distance in which the ball has to swing or seam and lessens the likelihood of your being adjudged leg before wicket (LBW, see Chapter 8) as the umpire will have more doubt as to whether the ball would have been certain to continue on to hit the stumps. After you have played the delivery it is crucial to remember that unless you are taking a run, you must get your foot or bat *behind* the line of the popping crease to avoid being stumped or run out.

Avoid being tempted by any width offered early in your innings. Leaving deliveries that are certain to miss the stumps enables you, without risk, to better determine the pace of the deliveries, the behaviour of the pitch and to assess any lateral movement.

THE LEAVE

When leaving a delivery:

▶ hold the bat to shoulder level at the completion of your backswing and step. To maintain a good batting position and to protect your wicket, your front pad should be covering the line of the stumps

▶ maintain a balanced stance and watch the ball along the entire path of the delivery

▶ do not commit to the leave too soon just in case the ball swings in late or seams back sharply

▶ once committed to the leave, ensure your bat and hands are held well away from the line of the delivery.

Figure 3.10 Position of the body when leaving a delivery.

Leaving the straight short delivery or 'bouncer' involves either swaying out of the way of or ducking underneath the delivery. When swaying or ducking out of the path of a short delivery keep you eyes focused on the ball and be sure to hold your bat and hands low and well away from the path of the ball.

Practice drill for leaving deliveries

Leaving deliveries should be practised just like any other batting skill. Using a tennis ball, have a partner throw down wide or short deliveries. Ensure you execute a backswing and step, maintain a balanced batting position and protect your wicket against unexpectedly sharp deviations by positioning your front pad in line with the stumps (though this of course

(Contd)

would leave you vulnerable to being adjudged leg before wicket, this strategy is considered preferable to allowing yourself to be bowled out). Develop this drill by asking your partner to randomly throw the ball straight and full towards the stumps so you will need to employ an appropriate batting stroke in order to protect your wicket.

To simulate short-pitched bowling have your partner throw a tennis ball underarm at pace at your chest or head height. Your aim is to sway or duck out of the way and to ensure your hands and bat are held low to avoid contact with the ball. This drill will also help to develop your reactions as well as provide you with greater confidence to face pace bowling.

Note: It is essential to wear a batting helmet for this drill.

Attacking pace bowling

Under normal batting circumstances your first priority must be to score runs so when a bowler 'over pitches' (by bowling a delivery of full length), look to get on your front foot and drive the ball to the boundary. The drives refer to all of the attacking batting stokes that involve a vertical downswing of the bat through the line of the delivery.

FRONT FOOT DRIVES

Driving deliveries of full length is considered a safe attacking option as the downswing of the bat is directed vertically through the line of the delivery making the timing of the stroke slightly less critical than if the bat is swung horizontally across the line of the delivery. When driving the full delivery the point of impact is also close enough to the pitch of the delivery to both minimize any significant deviation from the pitch and to ensure the delivery has not risen above the level (approximately knee level) where the ball can be comfortably struck with the middle of a vertically held bat. Driving the ball effectively is about timing and striking the ball cleanly with the middle of the bat. The best looking drives appear effortless in their execution so don't attempt to hit the ball too hard as good timing and the pace of the delivery will be enough to send the ball racing to the boundary.

The straight drive

The straight drive is employed to attack full-length deliveries directed on a line towards the stumps. When executed well, the straight drive results in the satisfying sensation of striking a perfectly adequate attacking delivery straight back past the bowler for a boundary four. The straight drive relies on timing and placement rather than power and is controlled throughout by the top hand. The bottom hand provides only light guidance to the bat, so ensure your bottom hand grip remains relaxed throughout the stroke.

To get yourself into the best position to execute a straight drive you will need to:

▶ establish a balanced position with a solid base
▶ complete your backswing and step by placing your front foot straight down the pitch just inside the line of the delivery
▶ maintain a steady and level head position in line with the delivery
▶ lean into the drive by straightening your back leg to help transfer weight onto your front foot
▶ make sure your head is over or slightly ahead of your bent front knee
▶ rotate your shoulders, arms and elbows to begin a vertical downswing of the bat
▶ raise the front elbow high to draw through and maintain a vertical bat swing
▶ accelerate the full face of the bat towards the point of contact
▶ watch the ball carefully then strike it directly below your eyes with the middle of the bat
▶ complete a balanced, straight and full follow through of the bat finishing with a high and bent front elbow position. The bat face should be facing the sky at the conclusion of the follow through.

The off drive

The off drive can be employed to attack full-length deliveries directed on, or just outside, the line of off stump. The ball is struck along the ground towards the area between the fielding positions of mid off and extra cover. The off drive relies on timing and placement rather than power and is controlled throughout by the top hand. The bottom hand provides only light guidance to the bat so ensure your bottom hand grip remains relaxed throughout the stroke.

To get yourself into the best position to execute an off drive you will need to:

▶ establish a balanced position with a solid base
▶ complete your backswing and step by placing your front foot just inside the line of the delivery and pointing towards the fielding position of mid off

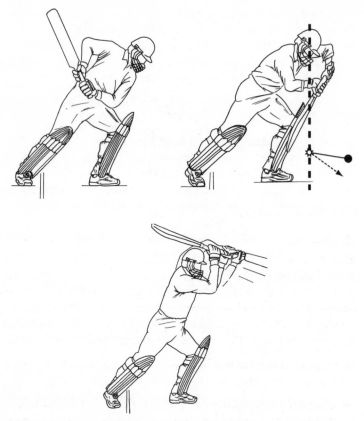

Figure 3.11 Body position for the straight drive.

- ▶ maintain a steady and level head position in line with the delivery
- ▶ lean into the drive by straightening your back leg to help transfer weight onto your front foot
- ▶ make sure your head is over or slightly ahead of your bent front knee
- ▶ rotate your shoulders, arms and elbows to begin a vertical downswing of the bat
- ▶ accelerate the face of the bat through the point of contact
- ▶ watch the ball carefully then strike it directly below your eyes with the middle of the bat
- ▶ complete a balanced and full follow through of the bat
- ▶ finish the follow through with a high and bent front elbow with the bat face facing the sky.

Figure 3.12 Body position after an off drive.

The cover drive

An elegant cover drive can be employed to attack full-length deliveries directed well outside the line of off stump. The ball is struck along the ground towards the fielding position of cover. The cover drive relies on timing and placement rather than power and is controlled throughout by the top hand. The bottom hand provides only light guidance to the bat so ensure your bottom hand grip remains relaxed throughout the stroke.

To get yourself into the best position to execute a cover drive you will need to:

▶ complete your backswing and step by placing your front foot across the stumps and pointing towards the fielding position of extra cover
▶ maintain a steady and level head position in line with the delivery
▶ lean into the drive by straightening your back leg to help transfer weight onto your front foot
▶ make sure your head is over or slightly ahead of your bent front knee
▶ rotate your shoulders, arms and elbows to begin a downswing of the bat
▶ angle the face of the bat slightly towards the off side
▶ accelerate the bat towards the point of contact
▶ watch the ball carefully then strike it directly below your eyes with the middle of the bat
▶ complete a balanced and full follow through of the bat finishing with a high and bent front elbow. The bat face should be facing the sky at the conclusion of the follow through.

The square drive

The square drive can be employed to attack full-length deliveries directed well outside the line of off stump. The shot is similar to the cover drive but involves **opening the face** of the bat with the bottom hand and striking the ball square on the off side. Because of the unusual wrist positions needed to execute the stroke the batter's arms cannot follow through in the same way as other front foot drives.

The on drive

The on drive can be employed to attack full-length deliveries directed on or marginally outside the line of leg stump. The ball is struck along the ground towards the fielding position of mid on. The on drive relies on timing and placement rather than power and is controlled throughout by the top hand. The bottom hand provides only light guidance to the bat so ensure your bottom hand grip remains relaxed throughout the stroke.

The execution of the on drive relies more than any other stroke on the batter having perfect balance at the crease. This is because to get yourself into the best position to execute an on drive you will need to take a shorter forward step than required by other front foot drives with your foot pointing slightly towards the leg side. You will then need to:

▶ complete your backswing and step by taking a shorter than usual step towards the line of the delivery. This shorter step allows the ball to be driven in front of the leading pad and for this reason the front foot rarely steps outside the line of leg stump
▶ maintain a steady and level head position in line with the delivery
▶ lean into the drive by straightening your back leg to help transfer weight onto your front foot
▶ make sure your head is over or slightly ahead of your bent front knee
▶ rotate your shoulders, arms and elbows to begin a downswing
▶ accelerate the face of the bat through the point of contact
▶ watch the ball carefully and strike it directly below your eyes with the 'middle' of the bat
▶ complete a balanced and full follow through finishing with a high and bent front elbow. The bat face should be facing the sky at the conclusion of the follow through.

Figure 3.13 Body position after an on drive.

The lofted drive

The lofted drive can be employed to stamp your authority over the fielding side by striking full-length deliveries over the top of the infielders into the unoccupied areas of the field. Depending on the line of the delivery the lofted drive can be struck anywhere between the fielding positions of wide mid on and cover.

The lofted drive is not a slog and still relies on timing and placement and is controlled throughout by the top hand. The bottom hand provides guidance and some extra power to the shot.

To get yourself into the best position to execute a lofted drive you will need to:

▶ complete your backswing and step by placing your front foot straight down the pitch just inside the line of the delivery
▶ maintain a steady and level head position in line with the delivery
▶ transfer your weight to your front foot establishing a balanced position with a solid base
▶ rotate your shoulders, arms and elbows to begin a vertical downswing of the bat
▶ raise the front elbow high to draw through and maintain a vertical bat swing
▶ aim to strike the ball earlier than with other front foot drives, i.e. directly below and ahead of the eyes
▶ accelerate the full face of the bat through the point of contact
▶ complete a balanced, straight and full follow through finishing with a high and bent front elbow position.

Figure 3.14 Lofted drive.   Lofted drive with power.

For extra power the arms can be extended through the point of contact. Your bottom hand supplies the power to the stroke but be extra careful to complete a balanced, straight and full follow through of the bat finishing with a high front elbow position.

Practice drill

You should practise all your front foot drives by placing a soft ball on a cone and driving the ball into a wall. Master the correct footwork and maintain a balanced follow though. Strive to strike the ball not fiercely, but well using the middle of the bat. Progress your practice by driving the ball while holding the bat with only your top hand. One-handed driving practice helps batters to develop a dominant top hand in the drives and also promotes a straight downswing of the bat. Use other cones or objects to designate target areas as a measure of successful shot placement.

THE BACK FOOT DRIVE

The back foot drive is my favourite attacking shot as you can employ the stroke to attack deliveries pitched on a good length. Depending on the line of the delivery the back foot drive is struck along the ground between the fielding positions of wide mid on and cover. The back foot drive relies on timing and placement rather than power and is controlled throughout by the top hand. The bottom hand provides only light guidance to the bat so ensure your bottom hand grip remains relaxed throughout the stroke.

Figure 3.15 Body position during a back foot drive.

To get yourself into the best position to execute a back foot drive you will need to:

▶ complete your backswing and step by placing your back foot parallel to, but deep inside the crease and in line with the delivery. Quick footwork is required of any batter attempting to play the back foot drive

▶ maintain a steady and level head position in line with the delivery and aim to get into a tall position high on your toes

▶ transfer your weight to your back foot and draw your front leg back to establish a balanced position with a solid base

- ▶ make sure your head is ahead of your back leg with your front shoulder dipped forward
- ▶ rotate your shoulders, arms and elbows to begin a vertical downswing of the bat
- ▶ raise the front elbow high to draw through and maintain a vertical bat swing
- ▶ aim to strike the ball at the top of the bounce
- ▶ accelerate the full face of the bat towards the point of contact
- ▶ watch the ball carefully then strike it below your eyes with the middle of the bat
- ▶ complete a balanced and full follow through of the bat finishing with a high and bent front elbow position. The bat face should be facing the sky at the conclusion of the follow through.

Insight

When driving the ball along the ground, your shoulders, arms with bent elbows and bat rotate together in the shape of a figure '9' (see Figure 3.16). It is important to rigidly maintain this shape throughout the downswing, contact with the ball and the follow through. Pay particular attention to maintaining a high and bent front elbow.

Figure 3.16

THE LEG GLANCE

The leg glance is employed to score from deliveries directed outside the line of leg stump and is a great shot to use to keep the scoreboard ticking over. The leg glance should not be the shot employed to deliveries either threatening to hit your wicket or passing outside the line of your body. The leg glance relies on good timing by using the pace of the delivery to deflect the ball along the ground behind square on the leg side (between the positions of square leg and fine leg). The leg glance is controlled by the top hand with the bottom hand providing only light guidance to the bat. The leg glance can be played on the back or front foot depending on the length of the delivery.

The back foot leg glance

The back foot leg glance can be employed to score from good length deliveries passing outside the line of leg stump. To get yourself into the best position to execute a back foot leg glance you will need to:

- complete your backswing and step by placing your back foot deep in the crease and outside the line of the delivery
- maintain a steady and level head position just outside the line of the delivery
- transfer your weight to your back foot and withdraw your front foot and hip inside the line of the delivery
- rotate your shoulders, arms and elbows to begin a downswing
- slightly angle the bat face towards the leg side at the point of contact
- strike the ball in front of your body
- wait for the ball! Don't push towards the delivery.

Figure 3.17 The back foot leg glance.

The front foot leg glance

The front foot leg glance can be employed to score from full pitched deliveries passing outside the line of leg stump. To get yourself into the best position to execute a front foot leg glance you will need to:

- complete your backswing and step by taking a shorter than usual step towards the line of the ball. This short step allows the ball to be struck in front of the front pad
- maintain a steady and level head position just outside the line with the delivery
- make sure your head is over or slightly ahead of your bent front knee
- rotate your shoulders, arms and elbows together to begin a downswing
- slightly angle the bat face towards the leg side at the point of contact
- strike the ball in front of your front pad
- wait for the ball! Don't push towards the delivery.

Figure 3.18 The front foot leg glance.

THE PULL SHOT

The pull shot can be employed to attack short-pitched deliveries arriving at waist height and directed on or outside the line of leg stump. The pull shot is usually played from the back foot and the ball is struck along the ground square on the leg side (towards the fielding position of square leg) making it an ideal boundary scoring option.

To get yourself into the best position to execute a pull shot you will need to:

▶ complete your backswing and step by placing your back foot across the stumps and into the line of the delivery
▶ maintain a steady and level head position in line with the delivery
▶ make sure your head is in front of your back leg
▶ transfer your weight to your front foot establishing a balanced position with a solid base.
▶ rotate your shoulders horizontally to begin a downswing of the bat
▶ swing the bat from high to low in order to strike the ball towards the ground
▶ accelerate the face of the bat and extend your arms through the point of contact
▶ watch the ball strike the bat directly in front of your eyes
▶ pivot on your back foot after striking the ball towards the leg side and draw your front foot back and towards the leg side
▶ complete a full and balanced follow through finishing with the bat face facing down.

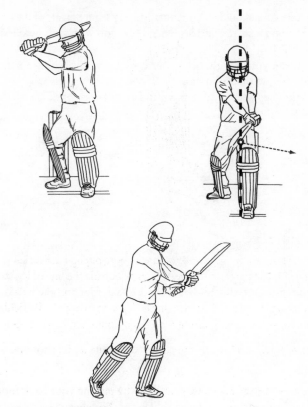

Figure 3.19 The position of the body throughout the pull shot.

On a pitch of consistent bounce, a version of the pull shot can be played as a front foot stroke by advanced, confident and well-set batters who are reading the length of the deliveries particularly early.

THE SQUARE CUT

The square cut can be employed to attack short deliveries directed well outside the line of off stump and is another terrific boundary scoring stroke. The square cut is played from the back foot and the ball is struck along the ground square on the off side.

To get yourself into the best position to execute a square cut you will need to:

▶ complete your backswing and step by placing your back foot across the stumps and parallel to the crease

- ▶ rotate your shoulders horizontally away from the line of the delivery
- ▶ maintain a steady and level head position with your eyes focused on the ball
- ▶ transfer your weight onto your back foot establishing a balanced position with a solid base
- ▶ make sure your head remains in front of your back leg

Figure 3.20 Executing the square cut.

- ▶ rotate your shoulders horizontally to begin a downswing
- ▶ swing the bat from high to low with your head and weight moving towards the point of contact
- ▶ accelerate the face of the bat and extend your arms through the point of contact
- ▶ strike the ball as it passes your body
- ▶ complete a full and balanced follow through.

THE LATE CUT

The late cut is a delicate and old-fashioned stroke that can be employed as a run-scoring option against short deliveries directed outside the line of off stump. The late cut is played from the back foot and uses the pace of the delivery to deflect the ball along the ground behind square on the off side. Many of the principles of the square cut apply to the late cut, the exceptions being that the ball will be played later and the shot can be employed against deliveries passing closer to the body than would be prudent to square cut. The late cut is an appropriate shot to play when the slips and gully have been removed to other positions so if the ball is struck in the air it will not pass close enough to any fielders to be caught.

To get yourself into the best position to execute a late cut you will need to:

▶ complete a backswing and step backwards and across the stumps by placing your back foot towards the line of the delivery and pointing this foot behind square on the off side
▶ maintain a steady and level head position with your eyes focused on the ball
▶ transfer your weight to your back foot
▶ aim to strike the ball just after it passes the body
▶ keep your head and weight moving towards the point of contact and watch the ball strike the bat face
▶ make sure that at the point of contact your hands are held at a higher level than the bat face in order to guide the ball towards the ground
▶ ensure your hands follow through along the path of the ball.

Figure 3.21 The late cut.

THE HOOK SHOT

The hook shot can be employed to attack rising short-pitched deliveries directed between chest and head height. The hook shot is played from the back foot and due to the high bounce the ball is struck in the air behind square on the leg side. This is an effective shot to combat and score off fast short-pitched bowling but it must be recognized that if there are fielders positioned at deep backward square leg, the risk of being caught out significantly increases.

To get yourself into the best position to execute a hook shot you will need to:

Figure 3.22 The hook shot.

- complete your backswing and step by placing your back foot deep inside the crease, across the stumps and outside the line of the delivery
- maintain a steady and level head position just outside the line of the delivery
- transfer your weight to your back foot to establish a balanced position
- move your hands to a high level and swing the bat from high so the ball has the greatest chance of being hit downward
- rotate your shoulders horizontally and extend your arms towards the line of the delivery
- make sure that contact with the ball is made with the head positioned just outside the line of the delivery
- accelerate the face of the bat and extend your arms through the point of contact
- watch the ball onto the bat face
- pivot on your back foot towards the leg side and maintain a full and balanced follow through, finishing with the bat face facing down.

Defending against pace bowling

Although the primary purpose of a batter is to score runs, innings of significance can only be built behind a solid defence. When you arrive at the crease the swing or seam bowler's intention should be to pitch their **stock delivery** on a good length in line with or just outside off stump. The safest method to defend a good length delivery that is certain to miss the stumps is to let the delivery pass without playing a batting stroke for the following reasons:

1 The ball arrives above knee level and cannot easily be driven with the meatier (middle) section of the bat, but remains below waist level so the cut or pull shots cannot be wisely employed.
2 After the ball has pitched, there will be barely an instant to react to any unusual bounce or lateral movement.

A good length delivery directed towards the stumps should usually be defended.

FRONT FOOT DEFENCE

The forward defensive can be employed to defend against any delivery threatening to hit the stumps and is also the safest technique with which to defend a yorker length delivery. The front foot defensive shot is controlled throughout by the top hand. The bottom hand provides only light guidance to the bat so ensure your bottom hand grip remains relaxed throughout the stroke.

To get yourself into the best position to execute a forward defensive stroke you will need to:

▶ complete your backswing and step by placing your front foot straight down the pitch and just inside the line of the delivery
▶ maintain a steady and level head position in line with the delivery
▶ straighten your back leg which will help transfer weight to your front foot and establish a balanced position with a solid base
▶ make sure your head is over or slightly ahead of your bent front knee
▶ rotate your shoulders, arms and elbows together to begin a vertical downswing
▶ raise the front elbow high to draw through and maintain a vertical bat swing
▶ decelerate the downswing of the bat towards the point of contact
▶ resist reaching for the ball but watch it strike the full face of the bat directly below your eyes.

Figure 3.23 The front foot defence.

BACK FOOT DEFENCE

A back foot defence is employed to defend against short and good length deliveries, directed on or just outside the line of the off stump and arriving at the batter between stump and chest height. The back foot defensive shot is controlled throughout by the top hand with the bottom hand only guiding the bat.

To get yourself into the best position to execute a back foot defensive shot you will need to:

▶ complete your backswing and step by placing your back foot deep inside the crease, parallel to the crease and in line with the delivery
▶ transfer your weight to your back foot
▶ maintain a steady and level head position in line with the delivery
▶ rotate your shoulders, arms and elbows together to begin a vertical downswing
▶ ensure that the front leg is drawn back and a tall position is taken
▶ raise the front elbow high to draw through and maintain a vertical bat swing
▶ decelerate the downswing to the point of contact
▶ watch the ball strike the full face of the bat directly below your eyes.

Figure 3.24 The back foot defence.

Defending against pace bowling may also involve avoiding a short delivery or 'bouncer' directed at your head or body. When avoiding a short delivery keep your eyes focused on the ball and sway away from, or duck underneath the path of the delivery. Keep your hands low and the bat away from the ball.

Batting against spin bowling

The fielding captain will often introduce a spin bowler or two later on in an innings as an older ball is worn and its abrasive condition is more likely to grip and turn when pitching. The short run up and a grip with fingers positioned across the seam of the ball may be your first clues that a bowler is attempting to spin the ball. By spinning the ball, spin bowlers create drift in the delivery then sharply turn the ball either into or away from the batter. To develop your knowledge of the variations within a spinner's repertoire it will help all batters enormously to study the section on spin bowling on page 106 and to discuss/practise your batting with different spin bowlers.

To successfully bat against spin bowling you must:

▶ quickly read the length of the delivery and get into a good position to strike the ball
▶ be patient – the longer you face spin bowling, the easier it becomes to play
▶ watch the spinner's hand carefully for changes in grip or wrist position that would suggest some variation in the delivery (see spin bowling)
▶ watch the ball along the entire path of the delivery
▶ avoid premeditating or committing yourself too early to any stroke
▶ think carefully before playing attacking shots to good length deliveries as any turn could result in you losing your wicket. When game situations dictate that you need to attack good length deliveries it is better to play straight and hit over the top of the infielders rather than slog across the line. This technique provides the greatest chance of striking the ball and controlling where it ends up.

Early in a spinner's spell of bowling be particularly watchful when looking to leave any delivery wide of the stumps. Acknowledge that you are unsure of how much the delivery may turn and that any delivery might turn some considerable distance. Therefore, if you are in any doubt as to which way or how sharply the ball will turn it is wise to employ a stroke to the delivery. Look to determine the pace of the deliveries, the behaviour of the pitch and aim to become better accustomed to the expected turn. From the onset of the spin bowler's spell attempt to score regularly in singles by using an angled bat face when playing forward or back defensive strokes to push the ball into gaps between the fielders. This strategy will force the spin bowler into mistakes in line and length that will allow you to employ more aggressive batting strokes.

FOOTWORK

A key technique employed against spin bowling is the nimble use of the feet to move a pace or two out of the crease to transform a tricky good length delivery into a comfortable half volley. When leaving the safety of your crease to slow bowling it becomes essential to make contact with the ball. Not doing so will almost certainly result in you being stumped by the wicket keeper.

When moving out, it is also crucial to maintain a good side on position to the delivery. This is achieved by bringing the back foot behind or up to the front foot. Avoid passing the back foot in front of the front foot as this action will create a restrictive front on batting position.

You can move down the wicket then, depending on your position, employ a front foot shot of an aggressive or defensive nature.

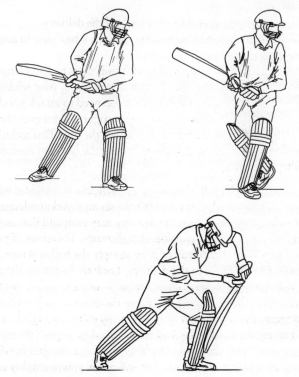

Figure 3.25 Good footwork is essential against spin bowling.

When leaving the crease do not move until the ball has left the bowler's hand. A good bowler who sees a batter stepping out will bowl a shorter, faster and/or wider delivery in an attempt to elicit a stumping.

Insight

Some batters occasionally fake an early forward step to encourage the bowler to think the batter is stepping out. The batter can then rock onto the back foot to play an attacking shot to the resultant **long hop** (short delivery).

Attacking spin bowling

In normal batting situations your first priority should be to score runs, so when the spinner bowls a delivery of full length, look to get on your front foot and drive the ball to the boundary.

THE DRIVES

When employing the drives to attack full pitched spinning deliveries, the principles of the stroke remain the same as when against pace bowling with the following considerations:

▶ the wicket keeper will be standing up to the stumps so unless moving out, part of your back foot should remain behind the line of the popping crease

▶ playing strokes against the spin of the ball is generally considered risky. For example, if a batter is attempting to off drive or cut a delivery that is spinning towards the leg side, the spinning ball can deviate and then pass through the gap left between bat and pad. Also, if a batter is directing towards the leg side a delivery that is spinning towards the off side, the ball is likely to turn away from the batter and striking the ball with a leading edge and into the air becomes more likely.

THE SWEEP SHOTS

The sweep shots are employed to score against good length spinning deliveries. The ball is struck along the ground square or just behind square. Well-executed sweep shots can cause heartbreak for spin bowlers who find themselves with no available length to safely pitch their deliveries. The sweep shots also have the advantage of scoring runs in areas usually left vacant of fielders when the spinners are bowling. As a result, the opposition game plan will be disrupted and their captain will need to rearrange their field to defend against the sweep and therefore create a gap somewhere in front of the wicket. But the sweep shots also carry risk. A cross batted shot played so close to the ground makes the judgement of any unusual bounce impossible and therefore a mishit from the bat's top edge becomes a distinct possibility. The sweep shots are played from the front foot and rely on timing and placement rather than power.

The orthodox sweep shot

To get yourself into the best position to execute a sweep shot you will need to:

▶ complete your backswing and step by rotating your shoulders horizontally up and away from the delivery and placing your front foot in line with the delivery

▶ adopt a low body position by dropping your back knee onto or very close to the ground

Figure 3.26 The orthodox sweep shot.

- ▶ maintain a steady and level head position ahead of your bent front knee and just inside the line of the delivery
- ▶ begin the downswing by rotating your shoulders horizontally towards the line of the delivery
- ▶ swing the bat from high to low in order to strike the ball towards the ground
- ▶ make sure contact with the ball is made with the head positioned just outside the line of the delivery
- ▶ accelerate the face of the bat and extend your arms through the point of contact
- ▶ strike the ball with the bat face slightly closed (angled towards the ground) and parallel to the ground
- ▶ watch the ball strike the middle of the bat directly in front of your front pad
- ▶ complete a full and balanced follow through of the arms.

Until mastered, the orthodox sweep shot is best employed only to good length deliveries directed on or outside the line of leg stump. However, with plenty of practice the shot can be employed to fuller length deliveries and to deliveries directed towards the stumps or even directed outside the line of off stump.

The paddle sweep
The paddle sweep involves swinging the bat down on top of the ball in order to strike the ball along the ground towards the fielding position of fine leg. Selecting to play the paddle sweep is appropriate when there are no infielders positioned behind square on the leg side. The paddle sweep gets its name from the fact that the action looks similar to the action of 'paddling' a canoe.

The slog sweep
The slog sweep is a lofted sweep struck powerfully over the fielding position of mid wicket. When employing the slog sweep, slightly open the bat face to create the necessary loft to clear any infielders and use your bottom hand to input some power into the stroke.

The reverse sweep
The reverse sweep is a modern shot that involves repositioning the bat to deflect the ball along the ground behind square on the off side. Your decision to employ the reverse sweep will be to exploit a gap

behind square on the off side. The benefit is found in the placement of the stroke and it is not necessary to strike the ball hard in order to score runs. The decision to employ the reverse sweep shot must be made prior to the bowler releasing the ball as the backswing must be checked to execute the shot correctly.

There are two acceptable techniques to get yourself into a good position to execute the reverse sweep shot. The first is by reversing the hands:

▶ check your backswing and place your front foot just inside the line of the delivery
▶ adopt a low body position by dropping your back knee onto or near the ground
▶ bring the bat forward in front of your body
▶ maintaining your usual grip and keeping the bat face towards the delivery, reverse the bat's position by rotating your bottom hand over, then in front of your top hand
▶ extend your arms down and towards the point of contact
▶ the bat face should be slightly closed (angled towards the ground) and parallel to the ground
▶ using the pace of the delivery aim to deflect rather than strike the ball behind square of the off side.

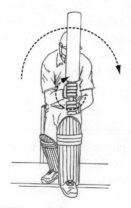

Figure 3.27 The reverse sweep.

The second method is by reversing the grip and this relies on similar principles to 'reversing the hands' except that the right-handed batter will quickly adopt a left-handed grip on the bat in order to deflect the ball towards the off side (left-handed batters will adopt a right-handed grip on the bat). The key to success with either technique is to place the back knee onto or very near to the ground and in so doing, adopting an extremely low body position.

THE PULL SHOT

The pull shot can be employed to attack short-pitched spinning deliveries. The techniques of the shot remain the same as when played against pace bowling except that when executing the pull shot against slow bowling, before striking the ball you will have the time to clear your front leg back and towards the leg side. This action will put you in an even better position to play the pull shot.

Figure 3.28 The pull shot.

THE CUT SHOTS

The square cut and late cut can be employed to attack slow short-pitched deliveries directed outside the line of off stump. The techniques of the cut shots remain the same as when played against pace bowling.

Defending against spin bowling

FRONT FOOT DEFENCE

The generally preferred method of defending against a spinning delivery pitched on a good length and threatening to hit the stumps is to smother the delivery before there is any chance of significant deviation. This is achieved by leaning or moving out towards the delivery and executing a forward defensive shot. The key principles of the shot remain the same as when played against pace bowling except:

▶ you have more time so you can lean or step further forward towards the pitch of a slow delivery than against pace bowling
▶ ensure you keep your bat and pad close together to avoid being bowled out 'through the **gate**'
▶ avoid pushing your hands towards the ball. Watch the ball strike the full face of the bat directly below your eyes
▶ ensure you strike the ball just in front of your pad since playing behind or level with your pad increases the chances of the ball 'ballooning up' and offering a simple catch to any close fielder.

Figure 3.29 The forward defensive shot.

BACK FOOT DEFENCE

Utilizing the full depth of the crease and employing a back foot defensive shot against a short-pitched spinning delivery gives a batter more time to react to any deviation between the pitch of the delivery and the point of contact. The key principles of the back foot defensive remain the same as when played against pace bowling.

....
Insight
Use 'soft hands', i.e. relax your grip on the bat when playing defensive shots to slow bowling. This technique allows the hands to absorb more energy from the impact and hopefully causes any unfortunate ricochets to drop short of the close catchers.
....

Dominating the bowling

An imposing batter will take the game to the opposition by scoring confidently and freely against the bowler's better deliveries while at the same time appearing to offer few chances to be dismissed. For example, an aggressive proponent of the lofted drive might quickly find the fielder positioned at mid off dropped back to the boundary. Taking stock of the revised situation, the intelligent batter, putting a high price on their wicket, now avoids playing the lofted drive and may begin stepping out and punching the ball along the ground towards the far flung fielder in order to score a few easy and risk free singles. Positive footwork is one method that enables a batter to attack the majority of deliveries while also inhibiting the bowlers' ability to settle into a steady line and length. When appropriate, employing the sweep shot or using an angled bat face to consistently direct the ball into gaps between the fielders achieves the same result.

Intelligent and dominant batting keeps the scoreboard ticking over, minimizes risk, creates frustrations for the bowlers, provides constant dilemmas for the fielding skipper and produces match winning partnerships.

Insight

Plan your innings in five or ten over sessions when batting. Setting short-term goals with your batting partner for runs or run-rates is a far more effective strategy than setting an overall target.

Running between the wickets

Running well between the wickets is a discipline which disrupts bowlers, frustrates the fielding team's game plan and often proves to be the decisive factor in a side's victory.

The principal techniques of running well between the wickets are covered below.

BACKING UP

The batter positioned at the non-striker's end of the pitch needs to be prepared to scamper through for any run on offer. When you are the batter positioned at the non-striker's end you need only keep your bat grounded behind the popping crease until the ball is delivered and therefore you should be positioned in front of the popping crease and walking towards the striker's end as the ball is bowled. This practice of 'backing up' creates forward momentum and gains a few strides for the first run. Hold the bat in the hand nearest the bowler so you can observe the bowler running in.

ANTICIPATION

Both batters should be watching the action and anticipating opportunities to take runs from defensive as well as attacking shots. Judging when a run is and is not available is largely a matter of experience. Under normal batting situations it is safer to err on the side of caution.

CLEAR COMMUNICATION

Running well between the wickets is unattainable without clear and incisive communication between the batters. If a batter strikes the ball in front of the wicket, it is generally the striking batter's responsibility to decide on the possibility of completing a run then incisively calling 'Yes!', 'No!' or 'Wait!' ('Wait!' is then followed by 'Yes!' or 'No!').

If a batter deflects the ball behind square on either the leg side or the off side, it is the non striker's responsibility to make the call. If at any stage either batter feels that the run is too risky, they must immediately and clearly call "No!"

Insight

It the ball has been struck only slightly behind square on the off side, it is the striking batter who is in the best position to judge any run.

When running between the wickets, batters should continue to communicate well by indicating possibilities and any intentions to run two or three.

SPEED BETWEEN THE WICKETS

Sprinting between the wickets maximizes the opportunities to take second and third runs and creates tension in the field and this pressure often results in fielding errors. Be ready to take advantage of any **overthrows,** so avoid running beyond the popping crease unless attempting to avoid a close run out attempt.

Run with the bat held in both hands to aid good balance, holding the bat handle in the opposite hand to the side of the pitch the ball has travelled. This allows you to maintain visual contact with the action during the turn at the end of each run. Swap the bat handle between hands after each run is completed.

When approaching the turn, adopt a low body position and reach out with the bat as far forwards as possible to cut down the distance needed to complete the run. Adopting a low body position will also help facilitate a speedy turn.

Run in a straight line and slide the bat over the line of the popping crease as just touching the line with the bat does not complete the run.

KNOWLEDGE

Identify, and in between overs discuss, the strengths and weaknesses of individual fielder's retrieving and throwing skills and exploit this knowledge when considering taking any runs. For instance, a well-struck shot directed towards a powerful thrower positioned at extra cover may preclude the chance to run what would be considered in most games to be an easy single.

ROTATING THE STRIKE

There are situations within a game where attempting to score with attacking strokes is not prudent. This may be due to a spell of good line and good length bowling, or when batters are playing themselves in or when a tail-ender wishes to give the strike to the last recognized batter. Under such circumstances the batters should discuss the situation then look to 'rotate the strike' by manufacturing quick singles with shots of low risk. The non-striking batter backs up well and the striking batter looks to nudge the ball into a gap in the field by playing the delivery defensively and with a bat face slightly angled towards the off side or leg side. With both batters set to sprint the single, playing the ball defensively and with an angled bat is the safest and most effective strategy for rotating the strike.

> ## Practice drill
>
> Bat as a pair and place cones at regular distance intervals around the edge of the area. The striking batter should practise executing some defensive batting strokes with a slightly angled bat face to place the ball into nominated areas. Make calls, sprint singles and practise rotating the strike.

Upping the run rate

With the innings coming to a close, with wickets in hand or a target to rapidly chase down, there are situations in a game when, in the pursuit of runs, the majority of your caution must be abandoned. This does not automatically signify that your wicket should also be thrown away.

When playing for boundaries, to give yourself the best chance of striking the ball well, be sure to:

▶ play each delivery on its merit. Remain relaxed, observe the delivery carefully and watch the ball right onto the bat face
▶ maintain a solid base, balanced position and sound technique throughout any attacking stroke
▶ look to move towards the pitch of deliveries to create half volleys
▶ bat to your strengths by using your favourite and most successful shots.

In conclusion, occupying the crease for lengthy periods will be essential to batting well and regularly building individual innings of significance. Preparation, concentration and shot selection are the primary skills that will dictate how successful you are as a batter.

Troubleshooting

Here are a few common batting problems and some possible solutions.

I MOSTLY GET OUT BY BEING CAUGHT BY THE WICKET KEEPER OR SLIP FIELDER

One possible reason for regularly being caught behind is that you are not getting your head in line with the delivery.

Solution: Whether you are playing a front foot or back foot stroke ensure that you have performed the necessary backswing and step to get your head in line with the ball.

Another reason is that your head is not steady.

Solution: It is much simpler to judge the delivery if your head is held steady. Try not to move until the ball has been released from the bowler's hand and then perform your backswing and step (whether forward or back) smoothly.

Alternatively, it might be that you are not watching the ball closely enough or you are not picking up the deviations in the delivery (i.e. swing, seam or turn).

Solution: Watch the delivery from the bowler's hand but appreciate that the ball may swing, seam or turn. Watch the ball closely along the entire length of the delivery and try to commit to your stroke a fraction later than you have been. Practise your ball watching skills.

I MOSTLY GET OUT BY BEING CAUGHT BY FIELDERS POSITIONED IN FRONT OF SQUARE

The problem could be that you are leaning back when playing your strokes and therefore your head is not over the ball at the moment of contact and you are resultantly striking the ball in front of your body and are unintentionally lofting your shots.

Solution: Adopt a lower body position by leading with your head when getting into line and ensuring that your front shoulder dips forward during the backswing.

I MOSTLY GET OUT GIVEN LBW

One possible reason for this could be that you are not well balanced when batting.

Solution: Ensure your batting stance and subsequent strokes are performed with good balance and that your head is moving into line with the delivery. Practise your strokes and hold your position at the end of your follow through to check your balance. Your body position was not stable or balanced during the stroke if you need to move your feet in order to maintain balance after you have completed a follow through.

Another reason for regularly being given out LBW is that you are not watching the ball closely enough or you are not picking up the deviations in the delivery (i.e. swing, seam or turn).

Solution: Watch the delivery from the bowler's hand but appreciate that the ball may swing, seam or turn. Watch the ball closely along the entire length of the delivery and try to commit to your stroke a fraction later than you have been. Practise your ball watching skills.

A third reason for being given out LBW (front foot shots) is that your footwork is not positive and the result is that you are attempting to strike the ball in front of your pads.

Solution: Take a more positive stride towards the pitch of the ball and strike the ball under your eyes.

I MOSTLY GET BOWLED OUT

A possible reason for regularly being bowled out is that you are not watching the ball for long enough or you are not picking up the deviations in the delivery (i.e. swing, seam or turn).

Solution: Watch the delivery from the bowler's hand but appreciate that the ball may swing, seam or turn. Watch the ball closely along the entire length of the delivery and try to commit to your stroke a fraction later than you have been. Practise your ball watching skills.

Another cause could be that you are employing the wrong batting strokes to deliveries.

Solution 1: Develop the discipline to defend deliveries that are likely to hit the stumps.

Solution 2: Present the full face of the bat when playing shots by attempting to hit the ball in **the V** (i.e. between the fielding positions of mid off and mid on).

A third reason for regularly being bowled out (to spin bowling) is that you are leaving a gap between your bat and front pad.

Solution: Be more positive with your front foot placement when stepping towards the line of the delivery. Ensure your front pad is positioned to cover the line of your stumps.

I MOSTLY HIT ATTACKING SHOTS TOWARDS THE LEG SIDE

Unintentionally hitting the ball towards the leg side is almost certainly due to a dominant bottom hand being employed in your batting stroke which acts to close the bat face during the downswing.

Solution: Ensure you are gripping the bat correctly with both hands held closely together just above the middle of the bat handle. Maintain a firmer grip with your top hand and relax your bottom hand grip.

10 THINGS TO REMEMBER

1 The role of each batter during the normal course of play is to score runs as quickly as possible without getting dismissed.

2 It is the captain's responsibility to decide the team's batting order.

3 Watching the game unfold provides you with much of the information needed to plan your own batting innings.

4 Adjust, re-check and re-mark your guard as often as you think necessary.

5 Identify the gaps in between fielders where the easiest runs will be scored.

6 Whatever the circumstances, it pays to 'play yourself in'.

7 Being balanced in your batting stance, with your head held steady and eyes level, makes batting easier.

8 Watch the ball all the way onto the bat face!

9 Leave wide deliveries and make the bowler bowl straighter.

10 Bat to your strengths by using your favourite and most successful shots.

4

....

Bowling

In this chapter you will learn:
- *the importance of 'line and length'*
- *the fundamentals of a good bowling action*
- *different bowling styles and an understanding of their relevant field positions*
- *how to bowl wicket taking variations.*

A gifted bowler does considerably more than just propel a cricket ball from one end of the pitch to the other. Though it takes a great deal of skill to consistently bowl the ball in the intended area, it also requires a measure of creativity and imagination to trouble the better batters. Accomplished bowlers challenge the batters by taking control of the cricket ball and making their deliveries behave in unexpected ways. Developing bowlers must learn how different grips, delivery actions and bowling styles affect how a cricket ball will behave as it travels towards the batter and as it bounces (pitches). Skilled bowlers can control a cricket ball to create swerve (swing or drift) in their deliveries, to achieve deviation off the pitch (seam) or to create unusual turn or bounce (spin).

The moment a bowler has developed some control of the cricket ball, the task then becomes one of anticipating the batter's intentions and bowling surprise deliveries referred to as 'variations'. A variation may be slower, quicker or may swing, seam or spin in the opposite direction than the usual (stock) delivery. A well-disguised variation is a key weapon in a bowler's arsenal and serves to sow seeds of doubt in the batter's mind.

Batters should also have a grasp of bowling techniques in order to help them predict what deliveries and variations to expect.

The ability of a batter to correctly predict or 'pick' a bowler's delivery or variation is an invaluable skill and studying different bowling styles is an essential part of a batter's development.

Line and length

The 'line' of a delivery is the measure of how far to the leg side or the off side the ball is directed, for example, an 'off stump line' is a delivery that would hit or pass over the batter's off stump and 'outside the line of off stump' refers to a delivery that would miss the stumps on the batter's off side. A leg side delivery would pass the stumps outside the line of leg stump but in most fielding game plans the majority of fielders are positioned on the off side of the field of play. The batter can therefore take a relatively risk-free swing at any delivery angled down the leg side and for this reason leg side bowling is usually a mistake.

The line of a delivery controls the width within which the batter has to operate and greatly influences which batting strokes can be correctly executed. Deliveries directed between the lines of off stump and just outside off stump pose an immediate question for the batters in their judgements of whether to play or leave the delivery. When bowling, make this '**corridor of uncertainty**' your primary target. Consistently bowling this 'tight' line presents the fewest opportunities for scoring and stands the best chance of taking wickets. Remember that **dot balls** (deliveries from which no runs are scored) create further pressure for the batters.

The 'length' of a delivery refers to the distance the ball bounces in front of the batter and varies depending on the bowling style, the pitch, the conditions and the batter. In the simplest terms any delivery described as 'short' arrives at the batter at or above waist level and encourages the batter to employ back foot shots such as the cut shot and pull shot. Deliveries referred to as 'full' or 'on the 'half volley', entice the batter forward and into playing front foot shots.

A delivery of 'good length' pitches in between a short and full length and just beyond the reach of the batter. The good length delivery will rise above the level at which the ball can be comfortably driven with the bat's middle (above knee level), but arrives at the batter below the level that back foot shots become obvious options (below

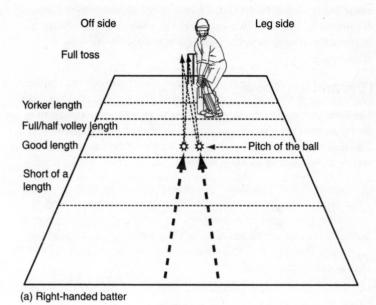

(a) Right-handed batter

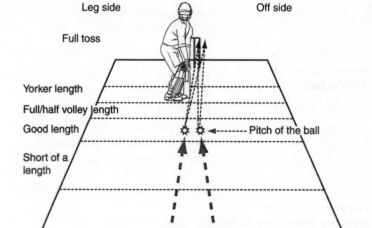

(b) Left-handed batter

Figure 4.1 Good line and length against right- and left-handed batters.

waist level). 'Front foot or back foot?' now becomes a tricky decision for the batter and the consequence of any uncertainty in a batter's footwork will be seen in the incorrect execution of the subsequent stroke play.

A delivery on a good line and length is directed to pitch then strike the very top of the batter's off stump and asks the batter to correctly judge the fine margin between whether to play or leave the delivery *and* then whether a front foot or back foot shot should be employed. The more questions the bowler poses with each delivery, the harder it will be for the batter to play effectively.

A consistently testing line and length places great demands of concentration on the batters and exerts pressure on their scoring. Improving your bowling will be largely about developing a consistently accurate line and length and although it is the batters who habitually receive the plaudits, it's the consistent bowlers who are more often than not the match winners.

Practice drill for bowling accuracy

Bowling accuracy can be developed alone by regularly bowling at a target marked on a good line and length or at a target drawn on a wall at the height of the stumps.

We refer to all parts of the body on the same side as the bowling arm as on the 'bowling' side, i.e. a cricketer's 'bowling foot' is the right foot for right-arm bowlers and is the left foot for left-arm bowlers.

All parts of the body on the opposite side to the bowling arm are referred to as on the 'non-bowling' side, i.e. the 'non-bowling knee' is the left knee for right-arm bowlers and is the right knee for left-arm bowlers.

Over and around the wicket

Bowling from 'over the wicket' means that the bowler bowls the ball with the bowling side of the body nearest the stumps, i.e. a right-arm bowler passes the left side of the stumps. Bowling from 'around the wicket' refers to the bowler bowling the ball with the bowling side of the body furthest from the stumps, i.e. a right-arm bowler passes the right side of the stumps. At the beginning of each spell the bowler must inform the umpire whether their intention is to bowl over or around the wicket and whether the ball will be bowled with the right arm or the left arm, for example, 'right arm over' or 'left arm around'. The bowler can decide to change from over the wicket to around the wicket, or visa versa at any stage but must inform the umpire prior to the change in angle who will in turn inform the batters.

The bowler's run up

The run up is the element of the delivery that allows the bowler to both maintain balance and provide momentum into the subsequent bowling action.

To ensure your run up remains repeatable and to avoid bowling no-balls, your run up must be consistent in both length and speed. Bowling a no-ball is effectively bowling a delivery from which you can't take a wicket and no-balls are therefore a bowler's worst enemy. Your run up will therefore need to be practised and measured during this practice as accurately as possible (usually in normal sized paces). Before bowling, pace out this required distance and mark it. The length of your run up will depend on the pace you intend to bowl and will be discussed within the different bowling styles.

From your bowling mark, start running with short steps and accelerate towards the crease by lengthening the stride as required to maintain good balance and rhythm. Ensure your run up is as comfortable, relaxed and as fluent as possible. This will be helped by holding your head steady with your eyes level and focused on where you want the ball to pitch. Smooth, balanced and rhythmic is the aspiration of all run ups. Remember that a run up may need to be repeated dozens of times each innings, so keep the run up economical by holding your elbows close to your sides and working or pumping the hands up and down in front of the chest.

The basic bowling action

For all styles of bowling the basic bowling action starts after the run up with a bound onto the bowling foot and into a good position to deliver the ball. This part of the action is commonly referred to as the 'back foot contact'. To do this effectively:

▶ keep your head up and maintain an upright body position during the bound
▶ hold the ball under your chin
▶ raise your non-bowling hand high and in line with the target
▶ make sure your front (non-bowling) knee is in a raised position when the bowling foot makes contact with the ground.

Side on action

Front on action

Figure 4.2 The back foot contact.

Whether you bowl with a naturally front on or side on action (or something in between), to avoid back injuries it is important to ensure that your back (bowling) foot is pointing in the same direction as your chest and shoulders.

Forward momentum progresses the bowling action from the bound and back foot contact through onto the non-bowling foot. This part of the bowling action is referred to as the 'front foot contact'. When executing the front foot contact the following should be applied:

▶ on contact with the ground your front (non-bowling) foot should point towards the target
▶ keep your head as steady as possible with your eyes focused on the target throughout the front foot contact and delivery
▶ start a full shoulder rotation by pulling your non-bowling arm down and through the line of the target

- ▶ execute a full swing of your arms and shoulders over a braced front leg
- ▶ release the ball at its highest point with a high and straight bowling arm
- ▶ the body smoothly follows through towards the target with both feet pointing towards the target
- ▶ keep your head up and eyes level. Maintain your balance and avoid running onto the protected area (see Chapter 8, page 168).

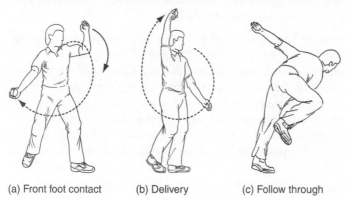

(a) Front foot contact   (b) Delivery   (c) Follow through

Figure 4.3 Bowling action.

Once the ball has been released the bowler should be ready to field off their own bowling by being prepared to accept any caught and bowled opportunity or to sprint towards the ball to prevent a run being taken by the batters. If the ball has been struck into the field the bowler should then hurry to take up a position behind the stumps (relative to the ball) ready to receive the return.

Appealing

Whenever you consider a batter should be given out (see Chapter 8) you have a responsibility to appeal to the umpire. Call loudly and clearly 'Howzat!' but be mindful that the delivery may not be dead and you may need to retrieve the ball or catch a return throw from the retrieving fielder. In reality, half-hearted appealing from a bowler can create the necessary doubt in an umpire's mind to turn down an appeal, so never be shy in your appealing. Bowling out a batter or having a batter obviously caught does not need an appeal in the first instance. However, if a batter is reluctant to '**walk**' (leave the field of play of their own volition) for some reason, then an appeal is required so the umpire can then adjudicate.

Pace bowling

Pace bowlers rely on beating the batter with the sheer speed of the delivery or by moving the ball laterally from the pitch ('seam'), and/or in the air ('swing'). The fundamentals of pace bowling apply equally to left- and right-arm bowlers.

The length of the pace bowler's run up largely depends on the pace of the bowler. A pace bowler's target speed during their run up should be the maximum achievable speed that still allows the bowler to maintain their balance and control within the run up and into the bound. A pace bowler's run up should be just long enough to economically reach this target speed a few paces before the crease. Too long a run up is a waste of a bowler's valuable energy and too short a run up will limit the bowler's potential to bowl at maximum speed. Remember to keep the run up balanced and smooth by keeping your head steady and by not trying to run uncontrollably quickly.

Leaning back slightly through the bound and back foot contact will produce greater momentum for the pace bowler and therefore greater speed through the release.

Extra pace is also generated by opening or 'cocking' the wrist before or during the run up, then flicking the wrist through the line of the delivery to a closed position as the ball is released.

The orthodox field positions for pace bowling are shown in Figures 4.5 and 4.6.

The right-arm pace bowler's stock delivery is bowled to the right-handed batter from over the wicket and is intended to pitch on a good length on or just outside the line of off stump.

The right-arm pace bowler's stock delivery to the left-handed batter is bowled from over the wicket, directed to pitch on a good length on or just outside the line of off stump and therefore angles across the batter. Due to this angle the wicket keeper and slips are usually

Figure 4.4 Leaning back produces greater momentum.

positioned slightly wider than against right-handed batters and square leg moves to a slightly backward position.

A pace bowler is proactively bowling for:

▶ the batter to miss the ball and to be either bowled out or adjudged leg before wicket (LBW)
▶ mishits and deflections coming from the outside edge of the bat and offering catches to the wicket keeper, the slip fielders and at gully
▶ mistimed drives offering catches to fielders at mid off, mid on and in the cover positions.

Pace bowlers can exert extra pressure on new, weak or defensive batters by repositioning:

▶ third man to third slip
▶ mid off to short extra cover
▶ square leg to forward short leg.

Pace bowlers routinely have a fine leg positioned to provide protection against the occasional delivery straying down the leg side. When further protection is required the captain and bowler may also consider:

▶ moving second slip to extra cover
▶ moving gully back to backward point
▶ moving cover and square leg fielders to deep (boundary) positions.

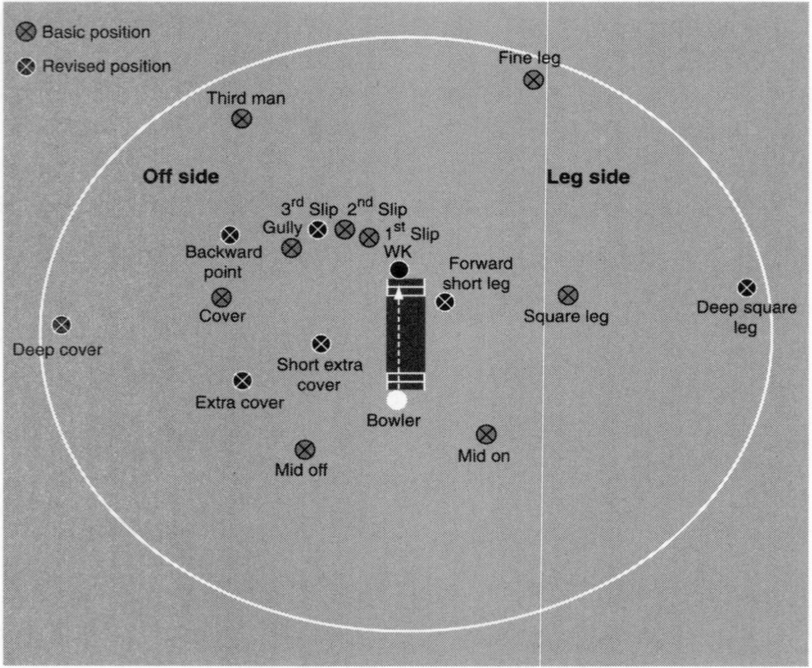

Figure 4.5 Basic field positions for pace bowling – right-handed batter.

Basic position
Revised position

Leg side

Deep square leg

Fine leg

Square leg

Forward short leg

Mid on

3rd Slip 2nd Slip 1st Slip
WK

Bowler

Off side

Third man

Gully

Backward point

Short extra cover

Mid off

Cover

Extra cover

Deep cover

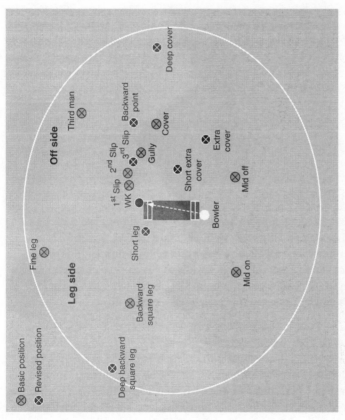

○ Basic position
● Revised position

Deep backward
square leg

Backward
square leg

Short leg

Fine leg

Leg side

Mid on

Bowler

Third man

Off side

1ˢᵗ Slip 2ⁿᵈ Slip Backward
WK   3ʳᵈ Slip   point

Gully

Cover

Short extra
cover

Mid off

Extra
cover

Deep cover

Figure 4.6 Basic field positions for pace bowling – left-handed batter.

SEAM BOWLING

Seam bowlers bowl at medium to fast pace – 65–95 mph (105–150 kph), and try to pitch the ball's raised seam on a good length to cause the delivery to deviate unpredictably from the pitch. The seamed delivery may deviate into or away from the batter. Seam bowlers want the batter to miss, mishit or edge the ball by committing to their stroke too early and down the wrong line.

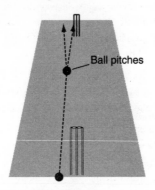

Figure 4.7 Seam bowlers cause the delivery to deviate from the pitch.

Seam bowlers are most effective early in an innings when the ball is new, hard and the seam is raised. Hard and cracked pitches are most receptive to seam bowling as the uneven surface adds to the unpredictability of the bounce while the ball's pace after rebounding from the hard surface is maintained. Green pitches also assist the seam bowler as the tufts of grass create an uneven surface although the softer surface can act to slow the ball down slightly.

When you bowl seam, aim to consistently bowl good length deliveries on or just outside the line of off stump, therefore forcing questions of the batter over whether and how to play the delivery. Variable bounce in a pitch means a good length is represented by a fairly large area of the pitch for the seam bowler, but on a flat consistent pitch a good length becomes a relatively small target area.

The condition of the pitch can change during an innings, so as a bowler it is important to continuously assess the pitch conditions as well as the strengths and weaknesses of the batter and to adjust your line and length accordingly. For example, you are bowling a fairly decent line and length and you notice that the batter has a dominant bottom hand and is trying to play almost every delivery towards the leg side of the field of play. Consider bowling a wider line outside the batter's off stump. This change in strategy will exploit the technical flaw by making the batter attempt to play towards the off side (apparently not the batter's favoured scoring area) or better still encouraging the batter to take risks by continuing to play shots towards the leg side from deliveries that are wholly inappropriate to do so. If the batter decides to shuffle across the crease in order to play the ball towards the leg side and is lucky enough to survive a few deliveries, a well-directed yorker on the line of leg stump will often capture the wicket. Remember that as a bowler, the more questions you pose with each delivery, the more difficult the delivery will be to play for the batter.

When seam bowling, the key to creating deviation as the ball pitches is by producing and maintaining a vertical seam position from the instant the ball is released until the ball hits the pitch. Make sure you:

▶ direct the vertical seam of the ball towards the target
▶ hold the ball between your index and middle fingers and the side of your thumb
▶ place your index and middle fingers behind the ball, either side of the seam
▶ hold your wrist firmly in an open (cocked) position.

Insight

When bowling at pace, attempt to impart some backspin by dragging your index and middle fingers down the back of the ball. Backspin helps the seam to remain vertical as the ball flies through the air.

Vertical seam

Figure 4.8 Batter's view of a right-handed seam bowler's grip.

Open or cocked wrist

Figure 4.9 Side view of a right-handed seam bowler's grip.

SWING BOWLING

Swing bowlers bowl at medium to fast pace – 65–95 mph (105–150 kph) – and endeavour to pitch their deliveries full in length to allow the maximum distance for the ball to swing in the air. The ball may swing into (in swing) or away from (out swing) the batter. The swing bowler wants the batter to commit to playing a stroke down the wrong line.

Swing bowlers are most effective either when the ball is new or when one side has been polished to a shine while the other side has been left to deteriorate naturally. Polishing one side of the ball encourages a delivery to swerve away from the polished side.

It is widely believed that it is moisture in the form of cloudy weather or humid atmosphere that creates the best conditions for maximum swing. Green pitches can also indicate some moisture just under the surface of the pitch so can assist the swing bowler too.

Under hot and dry conditions some pace bowlers can achieve reverse swing. This is a technique that creates swing in the opposite direction than would be considered orthodox, i.e. towards the polished side of the ball. Reverse swing is elicited when the ball is old by meticulously maintaining the dryness of the rough side of the ball and polishing the shiny side as normal.

When attempting to swing a delivery, aim to consistently bowl on a full length and direct the ball towards or just outside the line of off stump, therefore forcing the batter to decide whether and how to play the delivery. It is important to assess the strengths and weaknesses of each batter continuously and adjust your line and length accordingly.

An important aspect of effective swing bowling is producing and maintaining a vertical but angled seam position from the moment the ball is released until the ball hits the pitch.

Out swing bowling

An out swing bowler swings deliveries from a batter's leg side towards the off side and away from the shiny side of the ball. Out swing should be bowled on a fairly full length and directed to pitch on or just outside the line of off stump then straighten or swing away. Out swing bowling encourages the batter to play inside the line of the delivery and in so doing to miss or mishit the ball.

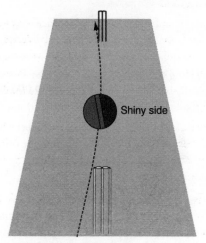

Figure 4.10 The line of an out swing bowl.

For an out swing grip:

▶ position the polished side of the ball on the leg side and direct the upright seam of the ball towards the fielding position of first slip

▶ hold the ball between your index and middle fingers and the side of your thumb

▶ your index and middle fingers should be behind the ball, held closely together on the seam.

Figure 4.11 Batter's view of a right-arm bowler's out swing grip.

The wrist position is the most important component in a bowler's endeavours to swing the ball. Hold your wrist firmly in an open (cocked) position and ensure that at the point of delivery, the palm of your hand is facing towards the position of first slip. You should notice that when the wrist is positioned correctly for out swing bowling only the side of your thumb will be in contact with the ball.

Figure 4.12 The wrist position for out swing bowling.

In swing bowling

An in swing bowler swings his deliveries from a batter's off side towards the leg side and away from the shiny side of the ball. In swing should be bowled on a fairly full length and directed to swing into the off stump. The lateral movement encourages the batter to play deliveries directed further outside the line of the off stump than would be usual and also exploits the gap some batters leave between bat and pad.

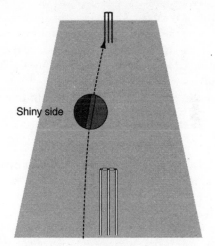

Shiny side

Figure 4.13 The line of an in swing bowl.

Figure 4.14 Batter's view of a right-arm bowler's in swing grip.

For an in swing grip:

▶ direct the vertical seam of the ball towards the fielding position of fine leg, positioning the polished side of the ball on the off side
▶ hold the ball between your index and middle fingers and the flat of your thumb
▶ your index and middle fingers should be behind the ball and positioned closely together on the seam.

The wrist position is the most important component in a bowler's endeavours to swing the ball. Hold your wrist firmly in an open (cocked) position and ensure that at the point of delivery the palm of your hand is facing towards the position of fine leg. You should notice that when the wrist is positioned correctly for in swing bowling, the base of your thumb will be flat against the ball.

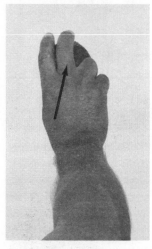

Figure 4.15 The wrist position for in swing bowling.

Insight

Experiment with the angle of the seam, your wrist position and grip to discover what positions create the most swing with your individual action.

PACE BOWLING VARIATIONS

When bowling at pace, a well-disguised variation from your usual or 'stock' delivery poses further challenges to the batters by measuring how well the batter is watching the delivery and testing their levels of concentration and technique. All your variations should be practised regularly and alongside your stock delivery to ensure that you have the necessary confidence to exploit these valuable wicket taking deliveries during your bowling spell.

The off cutter

The bowler uses his fingers to rotate the ball clockwise to deviate the delivery from a right-handed batter's off side towards the leg side. A tremendous variation for the out swing bowler and under perfect circumstances the batter's off stump is removed with no shot being offered to the delivery.

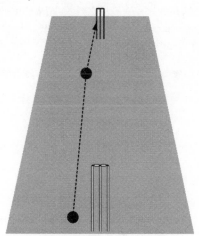

Figure 4.16 The line of an off cutter.

Figure 4.17 Batter's view of a right-arm bowler's off cutter grip.

When bowling the off cutter, the grip should appear similar to the bowler's stock (usual) delivery but the first finger drags or 'cuts' down the outside of, rather than behind, the ball. Off cutters should be bowled on a good length and directed to deviate into the off stump. When used as a variation the lateral movement encourages the batter to play outside the line of the delivery creating a bowled or LBW dismissal.

The leg cutter

The bowler uses his fingers to rotate the ball anticlockwise to deviate the delivery from a right-handed batter's leg side towards the off side. The leg cutter is most effectively adopted as a variation for in swing bowlers.

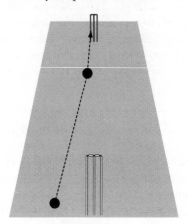

Figure 4.18 The line of a leg cutter.

Figure 4.19 Batter's view of right-arm bowler's leg cutter grip.

When bowling the leg cutter the grip should appear similar to the bowler's stock delivery but the first finger drags or 'cuts' down the inside of, rather than behind, the ball. Leg cutters should be bowled on a good length and directed to pitch in line with the stumps and straighten. When used as a variation, the lateral movement encourages the batter to play inside the line of the delivery and be bowled out or caught mishitting the ball.

The bouncer

The bouncer is an aggressive short-pitched delivery directed to rise sharply towards the batter's head or chest. It is an effective variation against a batter who has either shown an inclination for playing forward or shown fear or a lack of control when playing the short-pitched ball. In combination with an extra fielder positioned behind square on the leg side, the bouncer can also be used effectively against batters who compulsively hook the ball. Bouncers are most effective on a hard pitch as the ball will maintain its speed after rebounding from the surface.

The yorker

The yorker is a variation directed to pitch under the bat of the batter who is hesitant to play front foot shots and is often employed after a series of short-pitched deliveries. Even when expected, yorkers are notoriously difficult to score from as the ball is below the level where it can be driven with the middle of the bat. Yorkers are therefore useful deliveries to employ towards the end of an innings in order to restrict the batter's scoring.

The slower ball

The slower ball aims to confound the batter who has become accustomed to your usual pace. The key to the deception is that the run up and bowling action must be at the same speed as with your stock delivery. To take the pace off the ball, only the hand position or grip is different. Slower ball variations can be effectively bowled with a variety of different techniques:

- ▶ off cutters and leg cutters are effective slower variations
- ▶ the bowler's fingers can be spread much wider than normal
- ▶ the thumb can be positioned next to the first finger and held behind the ball
- ▶ the ball can be held more deeply into the bowler's palm than usual

▶ the wrist can be rotated outwards through 180° in order to release the ball with the back of the hand facing the batter.

Changing the angle

Changing the angle of delivery provides another useful variation. If your stock delivery is bowled from quite close to the stumps, an occasional excursion towards the edge of the return crease might prove enough to be the undoing of an unsuspecting batter who subsequently anticipates the wrong line. Be aware that to bowl a fair delivery your bowling foot is not permitted to touch the line of the return crease (see the pitch on page 3).

The most dramatic change in angle, though not a surprise to the batter, is achieved by changing from bowling over the wicket to bowling around the wicket (or vise versa). Remember that you must inform the umpire when you intend to bowl from the other side of the stumps.

Spin bowling

A bowler imparts spin on a cricket ball to create unusual behaviours in the air (drift and dip) and sharp deviation from the pitch (turn). The spun delivery may turn into the batter, turn away from the batter, bounce higher than usual or hardly bounce at all. Spin bowlers employ variations in the turn, pace, trajectory and angle of their deliveries to deceive the batter into missing or edging the ball.

Though spin bowlers can be effectively bowled at any point in an innings, they are most regularly used when the ball is worn as the abrasive nature of the older ball helps the spinning ball grip the surface when it pitches. Cracked and worn pitches are most receptive to spin bowling as the uneven surface adds to the unpredictability of the turn and bounce created by the spin. Damp or drying pitches also assist the spin bowler as the ball grips the softer surface better. The footprints of other bowlers can also provide excellent areas of **rough** ground for spin bowlers to target. Spin bowling should generally be bowled on a length intended to draw the batters forward and into playing front foot strokes, though it remains important to assess the various strengths and weaknesses of each individual batter continuously and adjust the line and length of deliveries accordingly.

FLIGHT

Flight refers to the trajectory of a spun delivery and can be varied to introduce further difficulties for the batter. Judging the length of a well-flighted delivery becomes a more complex task for the batter as the ball rises to a level above the batter's eyes. The well-flighted delivery also takes a moment longer to arrive and can upset a batter's timing.

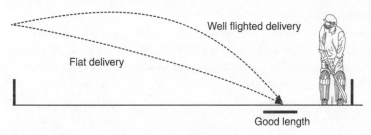

Figure 4.20 Different trajectories of flat and well-flighted deliveries.

DRIFT

Drift refers to any lateral movement in the air of the spun delivery. Unlike swing, drift is caused by the rotation of the ball and is accentuated by bowling into any available breeze. The spun delivery drifts in the opposite direction to the ball's rotation.

Insight

Find out from the following descriptions whether your natural action is to wrist spin or finger spin the ball. Practise by spinning the ball as hard as you can; your control will be developed over time.

Practice drill for spin bowling

Develop your spin by practising as often as you are able. Use any ball and practise spinning the ball hard. Spin the ball from hand to hand and then progress your practise by spinning the ball overarm against a wall. Experiment with your grip on the ball and identify what grip works best for you. Understanding the following orthodox methods of spin bowling is an important starting point, but many spin bowlers have become extremely successful with a variety of unusual grips, methods and bowling actions.

FINGER SPIN

Finger spin is generated by a bowler's fingers causing the cricket ball to spin in the air then alter direction when bouncing. Finger spinners often bowl faster and more accurately than wrist spinners and are well employed not only to take wickets but can also be useful to restrict run scoring when the state of the game requires economic bowling.

The orthodox grip

Hold the ball in the joints of your first (index) and middle fingers which should be well spread across the seam of the ball. This spread creates the purchase necessary for the first finger to effectively spin the ball.

At the moment of release, the ball of your palm should be facing towards the batter. The spin is generated by sharply dragging the first finger over and down the outside of the ball.

No thumb

Figure 4.21 Finger spin grip for right-arm bowler.

When bowling finger spin, your run up should be just long enough to economically accelerate to a comfortable and balanced gait a few paces before the bowling crease. Remember to run smoothly and to keep your head steady. Finger spinners often run up at a slight angle to assist in the spinning action. Bowl the delivery over a braced front leg and drive through with your bowling knee. Follow through with your bowling arm across the body.

Off spin bowling

A right-arm spin bowler uses his fingers to spin the ball clockwise, intending to turn the ball from a right-handed batter's off side towards the leg side. This turn, commonly referred to as **off break**, encourages the batter to play outside the line of the delivery and to be bowled out between bat and pad or to be caught mishitting the ball.

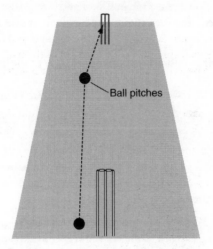

Figure 4.22 The line of an off spin delivery.

The field positions for off spin bowling are shown in Figures 4.23 and 4.24.

The off spinner's stock delivery to the right-handed batter is bowled over the wicket and pitches then turns into the batter. Therefore, when bowling to a right-handed batter an off spinner is proactively bowling for:

▶ the batter to miss the ball and to be either bowled out, stumped or given out LBW (leg before wicket)
▶ mishits and deflections coming from the outside edge of the bat and offering catches to the wicket keeper and at slip
▶ mishit cut, pull or sweep shots coming from the top edge of the bat and offering catches at short fine leg and at backward point
▶ mistimed drives offering catches at backward point, mid off, mid on and in the covers.

Off spinners can exert extra pressure on new, weak or defensive batters by repositioning:

- ▶ backward point into a gully position
- ▶ mid wicket to forward short leg
- ▶ extra cover to short extra cover.

Off spinners routinely have a deep backward square leg positioned to provide protection against the pull shot and sweep shot. When further protection is required the captain and bowler may also consider:

- ▶ replacing the slip with a deep mid wicket
- ▶ moving either mid off and/or mid on back to the long off or long on boundary
- ▶ moving extra cover back to the deep extra cover boundary.

The off spinner's stock delivery to the left-handed batter is bowled around the wicket and pitches, then spins away from the batter. Due to the angle and turn, the batter is more likely to play the delivery towards the off side. Therefore, when bowling to a left-handed batter an extra fielder is positioned on the off side at gully and the off spinner is now proactively bowling for:

- ▶ mishits and deflections coming off the outside edge of the bat and offering catches to the wicket keeper at slip and gully
- ▶ mishit cut, pull or sweep shots coming from the top edge of the bat and offering catches at short fine leg and at backward point
- ▶ mistimed drives offering catches at backward point, mid on, mid off and at cover.

Off spinners can exert extra pressure on new, weak or defensive batters by repositioning:

- ▶ extra cover to short extra cover
- ▶ backward square leg to forward short leg.

To left-handed batters, off spinners routinely have a deep backward square leg positioned to provide protection against the occasional short delivery. When further protection is required the captain and bowler may also consider:

- ▶ moving cover back to the deep cover boundary
- ▶ moving generally mid off, but either mid off or mid on back to the long off or long on boundary or both
- ▶ moving mid wicket back to a deep mid wicket position.

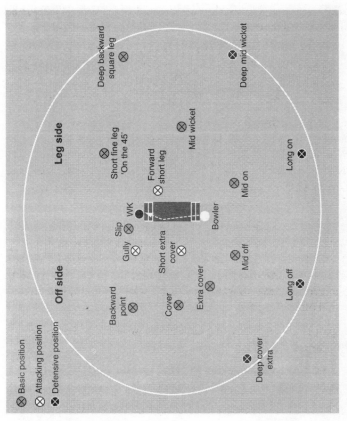

⊗ Basic position
⊗ Attacking position
⊗ Defensive position

Off side

Leg side

Deep backward square leg

Deep mid wicket

Short fine leg 'On the 45'

Mid wicket

Forward short leg

Short fine leg

Slip

WK

Gully

Bowler

Mid on

Long on

Backward point

Short extra cover

Mid off

Cover

Extra cover

Long off

Deep cover extra

Figure 4.23 Field positions for off spin bowling – right-handed batter.

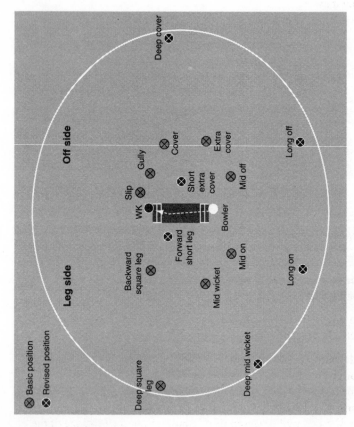

Basic position ⊗
Revised position ⊗

Leg side   **Off side**

Deep cover ⊗

Cover ⊗

Extra cover ⊗

Gully ⊗

Slip ⊗

Short extra cover ⊗

WK

Mid off ⊗

Bowler

Long off ⊗

Forward short leg ⊗

Backward square leg ⊗

Mid on ⊗

Mid wicket ⊗

Deep square leg ⊗

Long on ⊗

Deep mid wicket ⊗

Figure 4.24 Field positions for off spin bowling – left-handed batter.

Left-arm orthodox spin bowling

A left-arm spin bowler uses his fingers to spin the ball anticlockwise and turn the ball from a right-handed batter's leg side towards the off side.

Left-arm spin bowlers usually bowl around the wicket to right-handed batters aiming to drift the delivery into the stumps before turning it away.

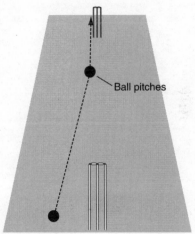

Figure 4.25 The line of left-arm spin.

The field positions for left-arm orthodox spin bowling for right- and left-handed batters are shown in Figures 4.26 and 4.27.

When bowling to a right-handed batter, a left-arm spin bowler is proactively bowling for:

- ▶ the batter to miss the ball and to be either bowled out, stumped or given out LBW (leg before wicket)
- ▶ mishits and deflections coming off the outside edge of the bat and offering catches to the wicket keeper, at slip and at gully
- ▶ mishit cut, pull or sweep shots coming from the top edge of the bat and offering catches at short fine leg and at backward point
- ▶ mistimed drives offering catches at backward point, mid off, mid on and at cover.

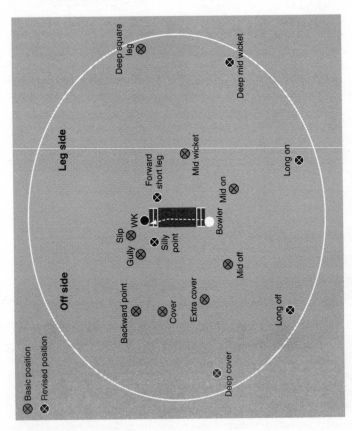

Figure 4.26 Field positions for left-arm orthodox spin bowling – right-handed batter.

Basic position
Revised position

Leg side

Off side

Deep square leg

Deep mid wicket

Forward short leg

Mid wicket

Slip

WK

Gully

Silly point

Backward point

Cover

Extra cover

Mid off

Deep cover

Long off

Bowler

Mid on

Long on

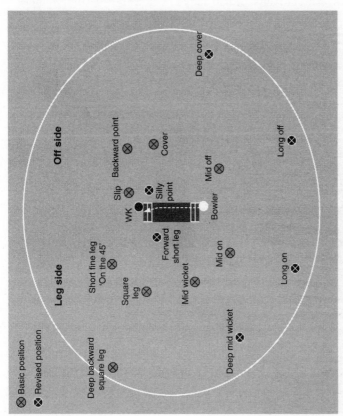

Figure 4.27 Field positions for left-arm orthodox spin bowling – left-handed batter.

Off side

Leg side

⊗ Basic position
⊗ Revised position

Deep cover

Backward point

Cover

Mid off

Long off

Slip

WK

Silly point

Bowler

Short fine leg
'On the 45'

Square leg

Forward short leg

Mid wicket

Mid on

Long on

Deep backward square leg

Deep mid wicket

The left-arm spin bowler's stock delivery to the left-handed batter is bowled over the wicket and pitches then spins into the batter. The batter is more likely to play the delivery towards the leg side. Therefore, when bowling to a left-handed batter an extra fielder is positioned on the leg side (from gully). The left-arm finger spinner is now proactively bowling for:

▶ the batter to miss the ball and to be either bowled out, stumped or given out LBW (leg before wicket)
▶ mishits and deflections coming off the outside edge of the bat and offering catches to the wicket keeper and at slip
▶ mishit cut, pull or sweep shots coming from the top edge of the bat and offering catches at short fine leg and at backward point
▶ mistimed drives offering catches at backward point, mid on, mid off, cover and at mid wicket.

Left-arm finger spin bowlers can exert extra pressure on new, weak or defensive batters by placing a close fielder at silly point and/or a short leg position and bowling some variations.

Left-arm finger spin bowlers routinely have a deep square leg or deep backward square leg positioned to provide protection against the occasional short delivery. When further protection is required the captain and bowler may also consider:

▶ replacing short fine leg with a deep mid wicket
▶ moving either mid off or mid on back to the long off or long on boundary
▶ moving cover back to the deep cover boundary.

Finger spin bowling variations

When bowling spin a well-disguised variation from your stock delivery can capture a wicket and should at least surprise the batters and let them know not to make assumptions about your bowling. To maximize surprise, it is essential to maintain an almost identical run up and bowling action as your stock delivery. All variations should be practised regularly alongside your stock delivery.

THE ARM BALL

The arm ball is the standard variation for the finger spinner. Once you have established that the batter should expect turn, the ball can be propelled off the first finger and released with no spin imparted.

This action will make the delivery swing away and also encourage the ball to bounce straight on. The hope is that any batter playing for turn will edge or miss the delivery.

Figure 4.28 Arm ball grip for right-arm bowler.

THE QUICKER BALL
The well-disguised quicker ball is a useful variation employed by the off spinner and is most effectively employed when the batter is new or attacking. Extra arm speed is the most often used technique of bowling the quicker ball but the approach and initial stage of the delivery action should be the same as with the stock delivery.

THE DOOSRA
A well-executed doosra should look similar to a normal finger spun delivery but will spin and turn the other way. This is achieved by rotating the bowling wrist, arm and shoulder through 180° (clockwise for a right-handed bowler) prior to release then imparting the spin with the back of the hand facing towards the batter.

CHANGING THE ANGLE
Changing the angle of delivery provides more variation. If your stock delivery is bowled from close to the stumps, an occasional excursion to the edge of the crease might prove enough to be the undoing of any batter who is not concentrating closely enough and subsequently anticipates the wrong line. The most dramatic change in angle, though not a surprise is achieved by bowling around the wicket (or for the left-arm bowler, over the wicket). Don't forget to inform the umpire when you intend to change the side of the stumps from which you bowl.

Very occasionally delivering the ball from a pace or two behind the line of the popping crease is another valuable tactic the spin bowler can employ to upset the batter's sense of timing.

WRIST SPIN

Many cricketers consider wrist spin to be the most difficult form of bowling to master. Wrist spin is generated by the combined effort of the bowler's wrist, arm, shoulder and fingers causing the cricket ball to spin in the air then alter direction when bouncing. Wrist spinners are useful wicket takers as they often impart faster revolutions and therefore often elicit sharper turn and more bounce than finger spinners. Wrist spinner bowlers can succeed with a variety of different grips, wrist positions and bowling actions. The key to your success as a wrist spinner will be experimentation and lots of practising to discover the most comfortable and effective method for you to spin the ball hard.

The orthodox grip

Figure 4.29 Wrist spin grip for right-arm bowler.

Holding the ball across the seam, grip the ball between the joints of your first and third fingers placed on opposite sides of the ball.

The ball should be held by the fingers and not be set in the palm of the hand. The middle finger and thumb rest gently on the seam to lend some support to the ball.

At the moment of release the palm of the hand is facing the batter and the spin is generated by rotating the wrist, arm and shoulder with a flick and snapping the third finger up the outside of the ball.

Practice drill for wrist spin bowling

Grip the ball in your bowling hand (palm facing away), then propel the ball across to your non-bowling hand by flicking your wrist and fingers over the ball. Try to make your wrist and each finger work hard. Develop your spin by involving your forearm, elbow and shoulder in the flicking action. Experiment with comfortable grips to establish how you can spin the ball the hardest.

When bowling wrist spin your run up should be just long enough to economically accelerate to a comfortable and balanced gait a few paces before the bowling crease. Remember to run smoothly and to keep your head steady. Wrist spinners often run up to the crease at a slight angle to assist in their spinning action. To elicit more spin, your bowling arm may drop slighter lower than perpendicular and follow through across the body.

LEG SPIN BOWLING

A right-arm spin bowler uses the wrist and fingers to spin the ball anticlockwise, turning the ball from a right-handed batter's leg side towards the off side.

The field positions for leg spin bowling for both right- and left-handed batters are shown in Figures 4.31 and 4.32.

The leg spinner's stock delivery to the right-handed batter is bowled over the wicket and pitches then turns away from the batter. Therefore, when bowling to a right-handed batter a leg spinner is proactively bowling for:

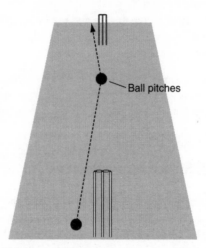

Figure 4.30 The line of a leg spin delivery.

- ▶ the batter to miss the ball and to be either bowled out, stumped or adjudged LBW (leg before wicket)
- ▶ mistimed drives offering catches at backward point, mid off, mid on and in the covers
- ▶ mishits and deflections coming from the outside edge of the bat and offering catches to the wicket keeper, slip or gully
- ▶ mishit cut, pull or sweep shots coming from the top edge of the bat and offering catches at mid wicket and at backward point.

The leg spinner's stock delivery to the left-handed batter is bowled over the wicket and pitches, then turns into the batter. The batter is more likely to play the delivery towards the leg side. Therefore, when bowling to a left-handed batter an extra fielder is positioned on the leg side (from extra cover) and the leg spinner is now proactively bowling for:

- ▶ the batter to miss the ball and to be either bowled out, stumped or given out LBW (leg before wicket)
- ▶ mishits and deflections coming off the outside edge of the bat and offering catches to the wicket keeper and at slip
- ▶ mishit cut, pull or sweep shots coming from the top edge of the bat and offering catches at short fine leg, square leg, mid wicket and at backward point
- ▶ mistimed drives offering catches at backward point, mid wicket, mid on, mid off and at cover.

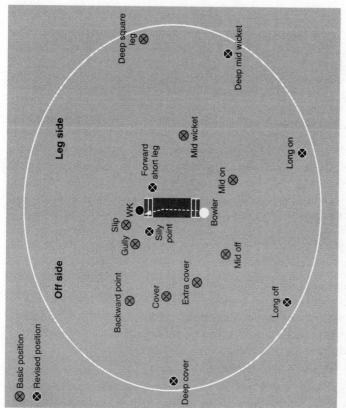

Off side   Leg side

⊗ Basic position
⊗ Revised position

Deep square leg ⊗

Deep mid wicket ⊗

Forward short leg ⊗

Mid wicket ⊗

Slip ⊗
Gully ⊗   WK ●
Silly point ⊗

Mid on ⊗

Bowler ○

Long on ⊗

Backward point ⊗

Cover ⊗

Extra cover ⊗

Mid off ⊗

Long off ⊗

Deep cover ⊗

Figure 4.31 Field positions for leg spin bowling – right-handed batter.

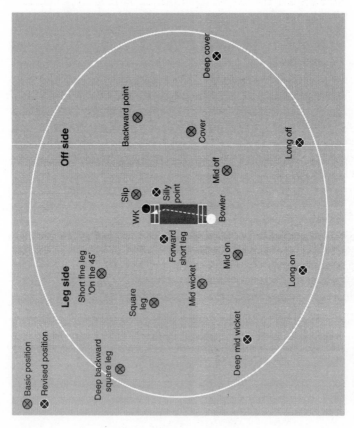

Figure 4.32 Field positions for leg spin bowling – left-handed batter.

⊗ Basic position
⊗ Revised position

Off side

Leg side

Deep cover

Backward point

Cover

Long off

Mid off

Slip

WK

Silly point

Bowler

Forward short leg

Mid on

Long on

Short fine leg "On the 45°"

Square leg

Mid wicket

Deep mid wicket

Deep backward square leg

Leg spinners can exert extra pressure on new, weak or defensive batters by placing a close fielder at silly point and/or forward short leg. They routinely have a deep backward square leg positioned to provide protection against the occasional short delivery. When further protection is required the captain and bowler may also consider:

▶ moving cover back to the deep cover boundary
▶ moving either mid off or mid on back to the long off or long on boundary
▶ moving mid wicket back to a deep mid wicket position.

Exploiting the rough

Leg spinners often choose to bowl to left-handed batters from around the wicket to work on the option of bowling out the batter through any gap left between the batter's bat and pad. Bowling around the wicket to left-handed batters also allows the leg spin bowler to attempt to pitch the delivery in the rough patches created by the footmarks of the bowlers bowling from the other end. Pitching the ball in these rough areas will create more unpredictable and variable turn for the left-handed batter to deal with.

LEFT-ARM WRIST SPIN BOWLING

A left-arm spin bowler who uses the wrist and fingers to spin the ball clockwise turns the ball from a right-handed batter's off side towards the leg side.

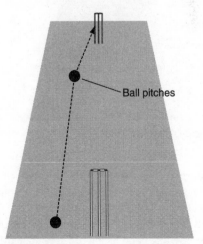

Figure 4.33 The line of a left-arm wrist spin delivery.

The left-arm wrist spinner's stock delivery to the right-handed batter is bowled around the wicket and pitches, then spins into the batter and therefore the fielding positions and wicket taking principles are identical to an off spinner.

The left-arm wrist spinner's stock delivery to the left-handed batter is bowled over the wicket and pitches, then spins away from the batter and therefore the fielding positions and wicket taking principles are identical to an off spinner.

Wrist spin bowling variations

A GOOGLY

A well-executed googly, commonly referred to as a 'wrong 'un', looks similar in action to a normal wrist spun delivery but intends to bamboozle the batter by spinning and turning in the opposite direction to the wrist spinner's stock delivery. The deceit is achieved by rotating the wrist, arm and shoulder through 180° in order to release the ball and impart the spin with the back of the bowling hand facing towards the batter.

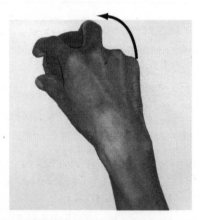

Figure 4.34 Batter's view of a googly (right-arm).

A TOP SPINNER

A well-executed top spinner looks similar in action to a normal wrist spun delivery, will not turn, but instead extra dip and bounce will be generated by the spin. Top spin is achieved by rotating the wrist through 90° and at the moment of release imparting the spin with the thumbnail of the bowling hand facing towards the batter with the seam of the ball held vertically and directed towards the batter.

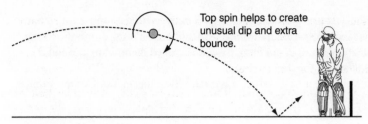

Top spin helps to create unusual dip and extra bounce.

Figure 4.35 The trajectory of a top spinner.

A FLIPPER

A flipper is back spun, should appear somewhat similar in action to the orthodox wrist spun delivery and should not turn. The ball will appear to float towards the batter, rather than dip normally, and then skid through low off the pitch. At the point of release the thumb is underneath the ball with the seam of the ball held vertically and directed towards the target. The back spin is achieved by the thumb flicking forward, underneath and spinning the ball in the opposite direction from that of an orthodox leg spin action.

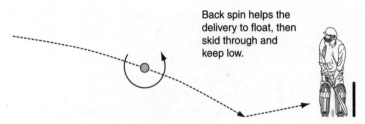

Back spin helps the delivery to float, then skid through and keep low.

Figure 4.36 The trajectory of a flipper.

Back spin can also be imparted on a cricket ball by rotating the wrist so the thumb is directly behind the ball at the moment of release and then releasing the ball with a normal leg spin action.

Back spun deliveries are often intentionally pitched on a shorter length than the leg spinner's stock delivery. This encourages the batter onto his back foot and into a bad position to deal with a delivery keeping low and shooting through.

CHANGING THE ANGLE

Changing the angle of delivery provides another variation. If your stock delivery is bowled from close to the stumps, an occasional excursion to the edge of the crease might prove enough to be the undoing of any batter who is not concentrating closely enough and subsequently anticipates the wrong line. The most dramatic change in angle, though not a surprise, is achieved by bowling around the wicket (or for the left-arm bowler, over the wicket). Don't forget to inform the umpire when you intend to change the side of the stumps from which you bowl.

Very occasionally delivering the ball from a pace or two behind the line of the popping crease is another valuable tactic the spin bowler can employ to upset the batter's sense of timing.

Whatever style of bowler you are, power, accuracy, variation, knowledge and confidence will be the fundamental ingredients to your success.

- ▶ **Power:** aspire to propel or spin your stock delivery with all the power you can control. Use practice drills to increase your power throughout your cricketing career.
- ▶ **Accuracy:** develop you accuracy by practising at every opportunity. Use a target and set yourself achievable goals.
- ▶ **Variation:** thoughtfully introduce variations in your bowling to deceive the batters. Practise all your variations alongside your stock delivery.
- ▶ **Knowledge:** knowledge is gained with study, coaching and playing experience. Learn from watching the professionals, read books, listen to your coach and get to grips with the roles, intricacies and tactics of the game by concentrating throughout every match.
- ▶ **Confidence:** confidence stems from the improved techniques developed from plenty of practice and is developed by the experience of success.

Troubleshooting

Here are a few common problems associated with bowling and some possible solutions.

I BOWL TOO MANY WIDE DELIVERIES

A possible reason for regularly bowling wides is poor use of the front (non-bowling) arm.

Solution: During your bowling action, ensure you raise your front (non-bowling) arm to a high position and your front (non-bowling) elbow is aligned with the target.

Another reason could be a lack of rhythm or balance within the delivery action.

Solution: Ensure your run up is smooth and balanced. An erratic run up will often lead to balance problems in the delivery, resulting in the collapse of the action and a lower than vertical bowling arm. Maintain a tall, high bowling action and follow through towards the target.

I BOWL TOO MANY NO-BALLS

A common reason for regularly bowling no-balls is a poorly prepared run up.

Solution: In the short term you should move your bowling mark back the necessary distance to ensure no-balls cannot be an issue during your bowling spell. After the game you will need to carefully re-measure the distance that you require to run in to bowl. Remember that your run up should always remain smooth and consistent.

Another reason could be an uncomfortably stretched delivery stride.

Solution: Ensure that your bound, back foot landing and front foot landing are all achieved comfortably. Do not stretch out with your front leg.

I STRUGGLE TO BOWL A CONSISTENT LENGTH

Bowling an inconsistent length is almost certainly due to an inconsistent arm position at the point of release. This can be caused by inconsistency within either the run up or the bowling action.

Solution: Practise bowling at a target placed on a good length on the pitch. Ensure both your run up and delivery actions are practised enough to become smooth and consistent.

I LOSE CONTROL WHEN MY BOWLING GETS ATTACKED

Solution: You will need to develop more confidence in your bowling action and abilities. Try not to dwell on the previous ball but instead plan your response with your next delivery. Develop the following unflappable routine to your bowling:

▶ as you turn to bowl, steady yourself, stand tall and take a deep breath
▶ decide what delivery to bowl and where
▶ check your grip on the ball
▶ run in smoothly
▶ focus on your target
▶ concentrate wholly on this one delivery.

10 THINGS TO REMEMBER

1 The 'line' of a delivery is the measure of how far to the leg side or the off side the ball is directed.

2 The 'length' of a delivery refers to the distance the ball bounces in front of the batter.

3 A delivery on a good line and length is directed to pitch then strike the very top of the batter's off stump.

4 To avoid injury and to aid consistency, it is essential to warm up your body in preparation for bowling.

5 To ensure that your bowling run up remains repeatable and also to avoid bowling no-balls, your run up must be practised, comfortable, relaxed and consistent in both length and speed.

6 During practice, experiment with the angle of the seam, your wrist position and grip to discover how the ball will behave with your individual action.

7 A well-disguised variation is a key weapon in a bowler's arsenal and serves to sow seeds of doubt in the batters' minds.

8 All your variations should be practised regularly and alongside your stock delivery to ensure that you have the necessary confidence to exploit these valuable wicket taking deliveries during your bowling spell.

9 Study batting techniques not only to improve your batting but also to help you identify and exploit the shortcomings of your opponents.

10 Power, accuracy, variation, knowledge and confidence will be the fundamental ingredients to your success as a bowler.

5

Wicket keeping

In this chapter you will learn:
- *how to approach the role of wicket keeper*
- *the fundamental skills of wicket keeping*
- *keeping wicket to various bowling styles*.

The role of the wicket keeper

The wicket keeper's primary occupation is to catch or at least stop any delivery that passes the batter. The wicket keeper is also alert to opportunities to dismiss batters by catching any delivery that has been edged by the batter (deflected from the edge of the batter's bat or from the batter's gloves) and to stump the batter that ventures beyond the safety of the line of the popping crease.

The wicket keeper must also receive the return throws from the fielders and, when possible, run out a batter. The wicket keeper is therefore the most important fielder in a side and a competent keeper behind the stumps is pivotal to the success of any team. Wicket keeping is also the most action packed and physically demanding position within the game and therefore high levels of fitness are required to avoid injuries and to provide the endurance required to remain at the forefront of a fielding team's high standards of effort and commitment.

COMMUNICATION

The wicket keeper is traditionally the team's chief cheerleader and motivator and is often an analyst of any flaws in the batter's technique. Best positioned to observe each delivery the wicket keeper also has a unique perspective in being able to detect information such as small changes in the condition of the pitch or the behaviour of the ball and is well placed to assess the dwindling energy levels of a bowler. Such observations should be quickly and discreetly shared with the captain.

Insight

Regularly praise the efforts of the bowlers and fielders. Maintaining team moral is an important role of the wicket keeper.

Preparing to keep wicket

To avoid injury, always wear the proper protective equipment when keeping wicket (see Chapter 10).

WICKET KEEPING WARM-UP

Keeping wicket is strenuous physical exercise. To be ready to receive the several hundred deliveries of an innings a wicket keeper should be fit, stretched and well warmed up.

It is a good idea to jog for ten minutes, starting slowly and increasing intensity. During this jogging, incorporate bursts of side stepping, high knee running, lunges and squats. Follow the run with a series of stretches focusing on the thighs, calves, groin and lower back (see Chapter 7). Have a team mate throw or hit you some catches. Start with some two-handed takes and then progress to one-handed catching, paying extra attention to your weaker hand. (For example, 20× two-handed catches, 20× dominant hand catches and 30× weak hand catches). Conclude your warm-up with a series of short sprints to get the feet moving well.

Insight

Practise your wicket keeping as regularly as possible with all the bowlers in your team. Talk to them to better appreciate how they are trying to take wickets. Pay special attention to the spin bowlers in order to better judge their turn and bowling variations.

FOCUS ON CONCENTRATION

Maintaining total concentration is essential for the wicket keeper. As wicket keeper you are involved in every delivery of an innings and the ability to be fully prepared to safely collect every ball and not to be distracted by the batter's shots or style is a discipline that must be developed.

Every keeper will have an occasional lapse in concentration and drop an easy edge or make the mistake of anticipating a batter striking the ball, not expecting the ball to pass the batter and subsequently missing the easy stumping. Keep these lapses to a minimum by getting into a fixed routine of firmly focusing your concentration on the delivery as soon as the bowler turns and prepares to bowl. During the delivery pay little attention to what the batter is doing and no attention to the batter's stroke. Wicket keepers must assume that every delivery will be missed by the batter and that the ball will need to be caught. The wicket keeper who is expecting the batter to strike the ball will not be ready when the ball actually arrives.

Standing up to the stumps

A wicket keeper is referred to as 'standing up' to the stumps when positioned within arms reach of the stumps and therefore within stumping distance. The presence of a skilled wicket keeper standing up to the stumps hinders the batter's ability to settle, both by restricting the batter's forward movement when attempting to drive the ball and by fermenting the fear that any errors will be punished. Standing up to the stumps is therefore an important skill to master and a competent wicket keeper will aspire to pressure batters by standing up to all but fast bowling.

SET-UP WHEN STANDING UP TO THE STUMPS

Wicket keepers are up and down in their stance on several hundred occasions during an average innings so to prevent avoidable fatigue it becomes essential that a keeper has a balanced, comfortable and relaxed set-up. To do this:

▶ ensure that you have a clear view of the bowler by positioning yourself half a pace behind the bowling crease and slightly to the off side of the batter
▶ your feet should be comfortably spaced approximately shoulder width apart
▶ adopt a poised crouched position but be mindful not to sit down and rest your weight on your heels. Sitting down on your heels will delay all your subsequent movements
▶ do not get into your set-up position too early – aim to be in a steady set-up position just a second or two before the bowler's

delivery stride. Getting down and into position too early will place an unnecessary strain on your legs

▶ balance your weight on the balls of your feet and lean slightly forward with the gloves in front of your body and resting lightly on the ground. Keep your hands together and relaxed with your fingers spread

▶ maintain a steady head position with your eyes perfectly level and chin held up.

Figure 5.1 Set-up when standing up to the stumps.

Insight

Don't get down too early or sit on your heels as this will hinder your primary movement and slow down your reaction speed.

Watch the ball!

Remember – Every other wicket keeping skill you employ is meaningless without firstly closely watching the ball from the moment it is released from the bowler's hand until the moment it strikes your gloves.

GETTING INTO POSITION TO TAKE THE BALL

Focus on the ball released from the bowler's hand, completely ignore any movements by the batter and assume every delivery will be missed. Maintain a steady and level head position, move laterally as necessary to get into position directly behind the line of the delivery. As the bowler is attempting to swing, seam or turn the delivery, commit to this lateral movement as late as your reflexes allow and only begin rising after the ball has pitched. Once the ball has pitched, rise smoothly with the bounce of the ball. Committing to a late movement will limit the need for you to make alterations in your position when the ball deviates.

TAKING THE BALL

To take a straight delivery bowled on or just outside the line of the stumps:

▶ maintain relaxed hands and hold the gloves together by overlapping your little fingers
▶ keep your hands low and in front of your body and present the largest possible catching area by splaying all your fingers
▶ point your fingers down for deliveries arriving below chest level and up for deliveries arriving above chest level
▶ don't snatch, grab at or move your hands forward towards the ball. Be aware that it is considered a no-ball if, prior to the ball being struck or passing the stumps, a wicket keeper moves any part of his body or equipment in front of the line of the bowling crease (see pages 3 and 164)
▶ watch the ball carefully and right into your gloves
▶ close the gloves around the ball as the ball arrives to avoid the ball bouncing out from your grasp, and to soften the impact allow your hands to give by collecting the ball into your body
▶ habitually pressure the batter once the ball has been caught, by moving your gloves, head and weight back towards the stumps.

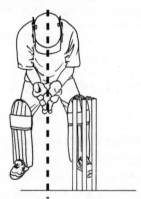

Figure 5.2 Taking the ball.

You will initially need to step sideways towards the line of the delivery when taking deliveries directed outside the line of the stumps. When you are moving laterally, try to keep your movements as smooth as possible, maintain a steady head and keep your eyes level. Hold your hands low and remember that two hands will always be better than one.

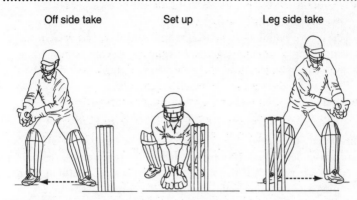

| Off side take | Set up | Leg side take |

Figure 5.3 When you are moving laterally, try to keep your movements smooth.

Taking the ball on the leg side is particularly tricky for the wicket keeper as the ball becomes hidden when passing in front of the batter. To collect leg side deliveries it becomes even more crucial for the wicket keeper to remain in a low position and to watch the ball bounce before rising. Lateral movement maybe necessary before the delivery pitches but endeavour to begin this movement as late as your reflexes will allow. Batters are prone to suffer a loss of balance when playing deliveries angled down the leg side so be ready to accept any stumping opportunities that are presented from leg side takes.

STUMPING

Once the ball is safely collected the wicket keeper will need to attempt to stump any batter that has ventured beyond the safety of the popping crease. To effect a stumping you must firstly collect the ball behind the line of the stumps and then shift your attention, head and weight towards the stumps and rapidly move the hand or hands holding the ball forward and through the stumps to break the wicket. Completely dislodging just one bail is enough for the wicket to be considered broken, though it is probably safer to dislodge both bails when making your attempt. The ball alone can break the wicket for a stumping if the ball is thrown at the stumps by the wicket keeper or if the ball bounces off the wicket keeper into the stumps and in so doing dislodges a bail.

Figure 5.4 Stumping.

As a wicket keeper it is crucial to be aware that the batter is considered out of their ground when the bat or any part of either foot is not grounded behind (not on) the line of the popping crease (see the pitch, see page 3). If you think you have been successful in your stumping attempt you should appeal to the umpire positioned at square leg with all the enthusiasm you can muster.

APPEALING

As wicket keeper you are the best positioned member of the fielding side to judge when a batter might be given out by the umpire when it comes to LBW, caught behind, stumpings and run out decisions. Whenever you are keeping wicket and consider a batter should be given out you have a real responsibility to lead the appeal to the umpire. Call loudly and clearly 'Howzat!' but be mindful that the delivery may not be dead and you may still need to retrieve the ball or catch a return throw from the retrieving fielder. In reality, half-hearted appealing from a wicket keeper can create the necessary doubt in an umpire's mind to turn down an appeal, so never be shy.

KEEPING TO SPIN BOWLING

Keeping to spin bowling is quite a challenge. A spinning cricket ball might dip or drift in the air, it may bounce unusually and or turn unpredictably, so concentrating on and closely observing the delivery is fundamental. Watch the ball along the entire path of the delivery and maintain a low position until the ball pitches. Moving late and quickly is the key to adept keeping to spin bowling. Hold your hands low and whenever possible get directly behind the line of the delivery.

Practise regularly with your team's spin bowlers in order to become better accustomed to the movement the spinners impart on their deliveries. Talk to the spin bowlers about their variations in grip and action and use this knowledge to better anticipate each delivery by closely observing and assessing the grip and action of the spinners as they run in and bowl.

When keeping to spin bowling, an unusually high bounce can be dealt with by clearing the outside foot backwards and towards the line of the delivery and twisting the body away from the delivery thus making the necessary room to take the ball to one or other side of your body.

Insight

When taking high-bouncing deliveries, hold your inside elbow tight into your body. This technique allows both palms to remain facing the delivery and therefore presents the largest possible catching area.

Figure 5.5 Taking a high-bouncing delivery.

STANDING UP TO PACE BOWLING

The more skilled the wicket keeper, the faster the bowling they are able to effectively stand up to and therefore all wicket keepers should aspire to competently stand up to the stumps to all but the fastest bowlers. This ability pressures batters by restricting their forward movements by remaining in a good position to attempt a stumping. Standing up is a particularly important strategy when the batter is looking to dominate the pace bowlers by moving down the wicket and hitting 'over the top' (of the infield). Standing up will invariably curtail this batting approach and cause the batter to adopt an alternative and more risky strategy to dominate the bowling. It is most likely that the batter will start playing shots across the line of the delivery.

STANDING BACK TO PACE BOWLING

Wicket keepers stand back from the stumps to fast bowling to give themselves the necessary time to react to quicker deliveries and to catch the edged deliveries that are a common mode of dismissal for batters facing pace bowling. The principles of the wicket keeper's set up remain the same as when against slower bowling except the set up position need not be as low as when standing up to the stumps.

When standing back from the stumps you should be positioned slightly to the off side of the batter with a clear view of the bowler and far enough back to catch at around thigh level any delivery pitched on a good length. The correct position will be dependent upon the pace of the bowling, the condition of the ball and the condition of the pitch. During a match identify this position quickly as the slip fielders will usually gauge their correct placement from the position of the wicket keeper.

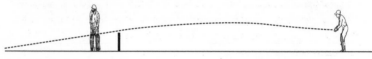

Figure 5.6 Standing back to pace bowling.

The principles of taking the ball when standing back from the stumps remain the same as when standing up to the wicket.

For deliveries that either drop short and are bobbling towards you or are arriving on the half volley, position your gloves together on the ground behind the line of the delivery and in front of your pads or body which act as a barrier to the ball in the event of a fumble.

Be prepared to dive in an attempt to catch or stop any delivery that is not directed close to you. When diving, get your head as far across and over your catching hand as possible to facilitate watching the ball into the glove. Dive horizontally, intercept the ball as late as you can and on landing try to roll onto your shoulders. Diving and then landing on your elbows will invariably jolt the ball loose.

Fielding as wicket keeper

As wicket keeper you will be expected to field any ball within your immediate area of the playing field. When fielding as a wicket keeper, remove and drop the glove from your throwing hand before retrieving the ball so that you can effectively throw the ball back towards the stumps.

RECEIVING THROWS FROM THE FIELD

When the batter strikes the ball into the infield or the outfield, the retrieving fielder should be trying to return the ball to the stumps as quickly as they are able. As wicket keeper, you are the primary target for all return throws so concentrate on the whereabouts of the ball, move immediately and quickly behind the stumps (relative to the ball) and to within comfortable arms' reach. With your gloves held over the bails, concentrate on the ball from the moment it leaves the retrieving fielder's hand until the ball strikes your gloves.

Ignore what the batters are doing as this may distract you from your primary purpose of receiving the ball. Vocally encourage the fielders to return the ball quickly to the stumps as this may restrict the batter's confidence to take a run. Try to make the fielding appear sharp and efficient by endeavouring to catch every return on the full and always lead the encouragement of the fielders by praising quick returns and accurate throws.

RUN OUTS

If the batters are running and there is the possibility that the return throw will arrive at the stumps before the batter can cross the line of the popping crease you will have the opportunity to effect a run out. With your gloves held over the wicket, watch the ball from the moment it leaves the fielder's hand and maintain focus on the ball right into your gloves. Don't look at the batter or shift your attention to the stumps before you have the ball in your hands as this will greatly increase the chance of a fumble. The instant you have safely caught the return throw, shift your attention, head and weight towards the stumps and rapidly move the hand or hands holding the ball back towards and through the stumps to break the wicket. To break the wicket when both bails have already been dislodged, remember that you can either replace one or both bails or, if there is no time to make these repairs, a stump can be pulled from the ground with the hand or hands holding the ball. The batter should be given out by the umpire if their bat or part of either foot is not grounded behind the line of the popping crease when the wicket is broken. If you are in any doubt to the running batters' positions you should break the wicket and appeal to the umpire positioned at square leg.

Once the action has finished and the ball is considered dead or has been called dead by the umpire, either toss the ball straight back to the bowler if they request it or more usually to a nearby fielder to start the process of returning the ball to the bowler.

Being involved in every delivery of an innings and rising to the challenge of being behind the stumps is great fun and doubtlessly one of the most exciting and rewarding aspects of playing cricket. Practise the correct wicket keeping techniques as much as possible so that you can better enjoy being the focus of your team's fielding efforts.

Troubleshooting

Here are a few common problems with wicket keeping, along with some possible solutions.

I'M NOT TAKING THE BALL CLEANLY

One possible reason for this is that you are not watching the ball for long enough.

Solution: Practise your ball watching skills with a partner or by rebounding a soft ball from a wall. When using a soft ball wear your wicket keeping gloves to retain authenticity within your practice. When watching professional wicket keepers, notice as they catch the ball how only the top of their head is visible due to them watching the delivery along its entire path and into the gloves.

A second reason might be that you are rising from your set up position too early.

Solution: Ensure your gloves rise with the bounce of the ball and not earlier. In addition, develop your reactions by practising making your first vertical movement only after the delivery has pitched. It sounds like this technique might make catching more difficult but in fact the reverse is true. When your eyes remain steady your brain will be able to better predict the path of the delivery.

Alternatively, it may be that your hands are moving forwards and towards the delivery at the moment of impact (snatching at the ball) and this is likely to cause the ball to bounce from your gloves.

Solution: To soften the impact ensure your hands are held together and in front of your body and then allow your hands to 'give' into your body when the ball arrives. You can develop this skill by practising with a partner or by rebounding a soft ball from a wall.

I'M NOT TAKING DIVING CATCHES

A reason for not taking diving catches is that you are not watching the ball for long enough.

Solution: see above.

Another reason could be that your set up position does not allow for rapid and early movement.

Solution: Ensure your set up position is balanced and poised. Make sure your feet are not positioned too far apart, that you are not getting down into your set up position too early and that you are not sitting on your heels.

It could be that your head is not getting close enough to the ball.

Solution: Dive towards the line of the delivery and try to get your head as far over the line of the delivery as possible. Remember that the nearer your eyes are to the ball, the easier it will be to catch.

Lastly, it may be that you are landing on an elbow and the ball is being jolted loose by this impact.

Solution: Upon landing gather your elbows into your body and try to land and roll on your shoulders. Practise this technique initially on a crash mat, cushion or other soft surface and develop the skill by then practising on turf.

I'M STRUGGLING TO CONCENTRATE

Solution: Form a process or plan to:

▶ Relax in between deliveries then switch on your total focus as the bowler turns to begin the run up. Relax again as soon as you are certain the delivery is considered dead or has been called dead by the umpire. Do not try to achieve the impossible by endeavouring to maintain total concentration for the duration of the innings.

▶ Never assume the batter will strike the ball. Truly believe that every delivery will be missed by the batter and will need to be caught.

10 THINGS TO REMEMBER

1 To avoid injury when keeping wicket, always warm up your body and wear the proper protective equipment.

2 The wicket keeper's primary occupation is to catch or at least stop all deliveries that pass the batter.

3 Maintaining team morale is also an important role of the wicket keeper.

4 Practise your wicket keeping as regularly as possible with all the bowlers in your team.

5 It is essential to assume that every delivery will be missed by the batter and that the ball will need to be collected.

6 Getting down too early or sitting on your heels will slow down your reaction speed.

7 Watch the ball from the moment it is released until the moment it strikes your gloves.

8 To better identify a delivery's trajectory, commit to the line as late as is realistic, then begin rising only after the ball has pitched.

9 Keep your movements as smooth as possible. Maintain a steady head, with your eyes held level. Hold your hands low and remember that two hands are always better than one.

10 Study bowling and batting techniques in order to anticipate ball behaviour and also to help you identify and exploit the shortcomings of your opponents.

6

Captaincy

In this chapter you will learn:
- *the roles and responsibilities of the cricketing captain*
- *the considerations and strategies a captain employs when batting*
- *the considerations and strategies a captain employs when fielding.*

All cricketers should read this section in order to get a better grasp of some of the tactics and strategies that captains employ during a cricket match. Improving your understanding of the captain's thinking will make your games more enjoyable, will create more knowledge within your team as a whole and could perhaps improve your own chances of taking charge of a team.

The captain's role

In no other sport does the captain of a team have so many varying and crucial duties. The cricketing captain is not only a selector, organizer and strategist but also needs the necessary character attributes to act as the team counsellor and chief motivator. In holding this collection of duties the captain of a cricket team bears the ultimate responsibility for the team's glories and disappointments.

TEAM SELECTION

Typically in club cricket, the team captain will select a balanced side from the best performing club members available. However shrewd the initial reasoning may feel, selecting too many bowlers or too many batters will only act to restrict a captain's ability to adjust the game plan according to the changing circumstances of the match. A balanced side consists of a combination of three or four pace bowlers, a decent spinner or two, an all rounder (a cricketer who is able to both bat and bowl proficiently), a wicket keeper and five or six specialist batters. Selecting a team with balance should give the captain the necessary resources to implement most changes in strategy that may be required.

Cricket matches are by and large won by the side that performs better as a team. In their singularity, individual performances are rarely enough to prevail. With this in mind cricketers should always be selected first of all on their level of commitment and then on their level of skill. A player with slightly less skill than another but with a significantly better attitude and sense of 'team' will always prove to be the greater asset.

ORGANIZATION

The captain should be well prepared ahead of every fixture. Club captains may be expected to either arrange the transport to the away fixtures or prepare refreshments and mark out the pitch at home. The captain should therefore aim to arrive before any other team member in order to greet the team, to start mentally readying themselves and the cricketers for the contest and in plenty of time to take care of all the necessary preparations for the match ahead.

A thorough team warm-up should be planned ahead of each innings (see Chapter 7). This helps to prevent injuries within the team and initiates the process of individual players commencing to function together as a team.

MOTIVATION

Different personalities will motivate a cricket team by employing differing styles. In his customary position in the slip field, the England Test captain Andrew Strauss appears a very calm and collected character who manages to bring out the best in his side by using only the most diminutive of gestures and expressions. On the other hand Graeme Smith, the South African captain, is often seen to be quite vocal and animated when commanding his national side. The common trait in these and all other successful skippers is their excellent communication skills when relaying enthusiastic encouragement, sincere reassurance and liberal praise.

Good captains quickly familiarize themselves with their team in order to communicate with each individual in a manner specific to bringing out the best in the player. Good captains are never aggressive and never appear to lecture, as doing so can only serve to alienate the captain from the players. The captain must also be seen to be fair and must avoid either overburdening the team's more unselfish members or favouring any demanding or dominant player.

Insight

Every cricketer gets a **duck**, misfields or drops a catch sometimes. Try to offer words of empathy and consolation. Demonstrating your annoyance towards an individual player is not the way to get an improved performance.

Whether batting or bowling the captain should endeavour to facilitate the sharing of pertinent information and observations. Listening to (but not necessarily employing) other players' ideas is a great way of making the whole team feel involved.

Individual players will need constant assessment and attention where necessary. A fielder who has dropped a catch may need to be fired up with a few encouragements, while the bowler who has just had a couple of marginal LBW decisions declined might well need to be somewhat calmed down.

After a game and depending on the result, players will sometimes be ecstatic and on other occasions, utterly despondent. Win, lose or draw, continue to motivate your side after the game by identifying, bringing out, then reflecting on the positives in the team performance and by highlighting the notable contributions from individual players. Offer a few words of encouragement to all your team before they go home.

Strategy before the game

As the match approaches the captain should settle on the initial game plan. The game plan describes the team strategy and acts as a vital asset to any team's motivation and success. The captain must first assess whether to bat or bowl if the toss is won and what strategy will be employed if the toss is lost. Most fixtures are limited to between 80 and 120 overs, so unless a dramatic change in weather conditions is forecast, the captain's decision whether to bat or bowl first (if the toss is won) will be made largely on their understanding of their team's strengths combined with the following factors:

THE MATCH FORMAT

Some league matches offer bonus points for batting first and this may influence a captain to elect to bat first.

THE CONDITION OF THE FIELD OF PLAY

A dry pitch can only deteriorate as the match proceeds and will usually give the side batting first the advantage. A dry pitch may therefore influence a captain to elect to bat first.

An even covering of green grass suggests the pitch will hold together and preserve the condition of the ball. Combined with a hard pitch, the ball should also maintain speed when pitching and may assist deviation from the seam. In these conditions, a captain with some high quality pace bowlers in the side may well elect to bowl first in an attempt to bowl out the opposition.

The browner the grass, the less seam movement should be expected and electing to bat first may become the captain's preferred game plan.

Strips of green grass running across the pitch indicate an undulating pitch and uneven bounce. An astute captain may be influenced to bat first before the condition of the pitch gets any worse.

Any moisture in or on the surface of the pitch will assist the bowlers in their attempts to swing and seam deliveries and as the pitch dries out will almost certainly assist spin bowlers. In moist conditions the captain may be influenced to field first so the team's bowlers can take advantage of the helpful conditions.

Damp grass in the outfield may act to hold up balls struck along the ground, making fielding the ball somewhat easier and making run scoring slow and arduous. Here the captain may be influenced to elect to take to the field first if they assess the outfield may dry out and the boundary become easier to reach for the batters.

THE WEATHER

Batting first on a scorching day is often the preferred (and both generally popular and usually widely supported by the team) game plan. Running around in the field under a blazing sun for several hours is obviously physically draining and makes batting afterwards considerably more difficult. This is especially true for the upper order who will need to be ready to bat as soon as the interval between innings has finished and are unlikely to be fully recovered.

A captain noticing cloudy and muggy conditions may be influenced to elect to bowl first if there are any quality pace bowlers in the team's attack. Moist overhead conditions are believed to assist the bowlers' attempts to swing the ball.

Many of these influences will be contradictory and make the captain's decision of whether to elect to bat or bowl first very difficult. A good captain won't hesitate to ask the opinions of the team's most experienced players but ultimately will have the necessary confidence to make their own decision, as right or wrong it's the captain who shoulders the responsibility for the eventual outcome.

Before the start of a cricket match the away captain calls the toss of a coin. The winner of the toss then elects whether to bat or bowl first. Whether the toss is won or lost a team talk is held and the relevant aspect of the game plan is shared. At this time the captain's comments should be kept simple and focus on the task in hand.

Strategy when batting

It is the captain's responsibility to decide the batting order of the team's 11 players. If the captain wishes, the batting order can be shuffled at any time during the batting innings to take into account any change in the game plan or the position of the innings.

The opening batters should proceed to the middle with a clear understanding of their responsibilities. The captain's batting orders to the openers usually consist of a few choice phrases concerning the advantage of a solid start to the team's batting effort, seeing off the new ball, good running between the wickets and the importance of the team game plan.

A good captain will encourage the whole team to watch the innings together, will lead the support for the batters and greet each returning batter with the appropriate dose of encouragement or praise. The captain may also choose to brief each new batter as the innings progresses. Depending on the state of the game, the instructions may be for the batter to play their 'natural game', to get their head down and play defensively, to allow the established batter to take the majority of the strike or to have a quick look then hit out aggressively. Tail enders will often be reminded to play 'properly' since their wicket and runs at the end of an innings are just as valuable to the team efforts as runs struck but the openers. Irrespective of their position within the batting order, the captain's own innings is obliged to reflect discipline and all of the standards expected of the other players.

Insight

Encourage batters to plan their innings in five or ten over sessions. Setting short-term goals for runs or run-rates is a far more effective strategy than setting an overall target.

Strategy when fielding

Leading a team onto the field of play can be one of the proudest moments within the sport of cricket. The captain will already have an idea of which bowlers will bowl in what order and from which end. This initial game plan has taken into account the captain's own knowledge of the bowlers, the conditions of the pitch and the state of the game.

Every player must be aware of the initial game plan and last-minute instructions are given to the team collectively in the dressing room or in a huddle on the field. The captain informs the opening bowlers of their task and dispatches them to warm up together. It can be sensible for the captain to split the fielding warm-up between the infielders and the outfielders. The infielders will practise their close catching to elevate their levels of concentration and hand-eye co-ordination while the outfielders revive their retrieving and throwing skills as well as taking a few towering catches.

All fielders should be instructed to keep an eye on their captain in case any adjustments in the game plan need communicating and for when changes to fielding positions are required. A team who keep in touch with regular eye contact enables the captain to make subtle adjustments to the field as well as reinforcing the team's concentration and allowing for less vocal shows of disapproval, encouragement or praise.

A fielding captain's primary ambition is to dismiss the opposition side for as few runs as possible and although opening with spin can be a cunning ploy, the new ball will be hard and polished (best for swing and seam bowling), so it is the pace bowlers who are usually tossed the new ball. This opening period of play is critical to the success of the fielding team's game plan as a few early wickets can place the initiative firmly with the fielding side while a succession of boundaries will set the opposition off to a flying start. Therefore, the opening pair of bowlers will generally be the best bowlers at the captain's disposal and are referred to as strike bowlers. Strike bowlers are the bowlers within a side who are considered most likely to take wickets.

The team's bowlers should be encouraged to be knowledgeable of their art and assist in the setting of the field but it is ultimately the captain who positions the field, opts to use attacking or defensive fielding strategies and decides who fields where.

Assessment of individual fielders' prowess should be considered when setting the field, and appropriate positions chosen for the better and weaker fielders in a side. The captain should try to avoid making any player walk too far in between overs (for example, fine leg to fine leg) without good cause and a few sympathetic words. Captains should neither ask a player to field closer to the bat than they are comfortable with nor without the necessary protective equipment.

Ideally the captain sets a field which will both complement the bowlers in their endeavours to take wickets and also act to restrict the flow of runs. Unfortunately these two ambitions don't necessarily go hand in hand, and a captain must regularly either sacrifice runs in the pursuit of wickets or risk taking fewer wickets to restrict the batters scoring runs. This balance of attack and defence largely depends on the skill and abilities of each bowler. When a captain employs a high quality opening bowler who has the necessary skill to trouble the batters, an attacking field can be confidently set with several more close catchers introduced into positions to exert further pressure on the batters. However, if the batters are relatively untroubled and runs are being scored too freely, some fielders will need to be repositioned towards the boundary to restrict the scoring.

Captains are most often found fielding in the positions of mid off or first slip. These particular infield positions allow for the captain to remain in close communication with the bowlers and the wicket keeper, as well as providing an adequate view of the deliveries. The captain should pay special consideration to the opinions of an experienced wicket keeper as it is the wicket keeper who is best positioned to assess the bowling and also well placed to offer to the captain a useful analysis of the batting.

Shining just one side of the ball will encourage the delivery to swing so within a few overs of taking to the field the opening bowlers and the captain must decide which side of the ball will be polished and which side will be left to deteriorate naturally. Just like a coin, a cricket ball carries a different design on each side. For example, a cricket ball manufactured by Readers, Dukes or Kookaburra have their brand logos printed on one side of the ball and it is this side that would be referred to as the 'Readers', 'Dukes' or Kookaburra' side. Every fielder should be made aware of the decision and of which team member has been designated the 'ball-shiner'. The ball-shiner is the individual who gives the shiny side of the ball a quick polish when returning it to the bowler.

The captain should think to immediately reposition fielders when an individual batter either shows a propensity for one particular stroke or strikes the ball predominantly towards one particular area of the playing field. Fielders can be repositioned to either discourage the batter from playing their favoured stroke or with the intention of encouraging the batter's favoured stroke but asking the bowler to adjust the line and/or length of the deliveries to ensure the governing stroke carries significantly more risk. For example, a batter whose bottom hand dominates their stroke-play will usually hit the ball towards the leg side. This flaw in batting technique can be exploited by repositioning an extra fielder or two to the leg side, therefore restricting the batter's favoured run scoring option and encouraging the batter to play strokes towards the off side where they are less likely to be confidently executed. A dominant bottom hand can equally be exposed by totally vacating the mid wicket area of fielders, thus creating an attractive area for the batter to target and then asking the bowler to bowl deliveries on a line directed consistently outside the line of off stump. Attempting to strike deliveries bowled outside the line of off stump towards the leg side of the playing field is almost always a misguided approach that carries enormous risk for the batter. Employing such fielding strategies and ploys serves to create a wicket taking opportunity and to stem the scoring of runs as the captain's game plan has been intelligently adjusted to exploit an individual batter's weakness.

Building pressure on the batters is achieved primarily by bowlers bowling good line and length but the captain will also need to change the bowlers so that batters cannot get familiar with one particular bowler or style. The captain must therefore know his bowlers well in order to decide when each bowler will bowl and how many overs should be bowled by each bowler in each spell. The captain should inform a bowler at least five minutes before they are due to bowl in order to allow the bowler to both mentally prepare and physically warm up for the task.

From the first ball, the successful captain continuously assesses and reacts to the conditions, the bowling and the batting by immediately adjusting the game plan and field positions accordingly. Astute captains always work to a plan but do not work to a fixed plan. Bowlers will be changed and fielders brought closer to defensive batters and placed deeper for proficient stroke-players. Flexibility in the application of the available resources is a key facet of a successful captain though the captain should also be mindful to ensure that the innings proceeds at a brisk pace. Too much time spent making changes will not only upset the batters and the umpires but can also de-motivate the fielding side. The captain should conduct further team talks at least once a session as this allows the ever-changing game plan to be well communicated and any new ideas aired.

Never let an innings drift. If the innings is not going to the game plan then the strategy should be changed immediately. Enterprising ploys and maintaining a fluid field can often be used to secure wickets. Suddenly, and for no apparent reason, placing a fielder close and perhaps in the batter's eye line can disrupt a settled batter. Leaving a gap in the field square of the batter may encourage a well-set batter to abandon his sound and proven technique of playing straight with a vertical bat face and striking the ball in the V. The temptation will be for the batter to start playing more risky strokes across the line of the delivery in his attempt to exploit the gap.

When deliveries are seaming or swinging captains can attempt to draw the batter onto the front foot by removing the extra cover fielder and encouraging the drive. A batter is more likely to edge a deviating delivery when driving at the ball with a vertically held bat face, so the extra cover fielder is most likely to be repositioned into the **slip cordon** or at the position of gully.

The astute captain has almost certainly ensured that the team's most experienced two bowlers can bowl the final few overs of an innings when the batters will be at their most aggressive. The game will be in one of two states: wickets will be required to win the game or runs will need to be restricted to avoid the loss. Aggressive bowling to a ring of close fielders gives the fielding team the best chance of bowling out the tail, while tight yorker length bowling with the maximum permitted number of fielders (see match formats on page 7) positioned back on the boundary attempts to restrict runs.

However late in the day it is and however hopeless the team's position appears, the state of a cricket match can change in the blinking of an eye and score books are strewn with the most unlikely of results. The captain must always appear to hold onto this belief and be seen to have the wherewithal to bring off the victory.

The mental attitude of a team undoubtedly follows the captain's lead. Therefore the captain must demonstrate significant efforts in the crucial areas of concentration, commitment and fielding standards. The captain is also duty bound to ensure that all play is conducted within the Spirit of the Game as well as within the Laws.

Important note on safety

If two or more fielders are converging under a catch or call for the same ball, it becomes the captain's responsibility to immediately identify which fielder holds the best position to make the catch and to clearly call that fielder's name. The other fielder must immediately pull out of the attempt.

After the game

Win, lose or draw the captain should lead their team in remaining magnanimous towards all the players and officials who were involved in the fixture. It is expected that the captains and teams get together to exchange social pleasantries and those whose efforts have contributed to the day should be acknowledged. Congratulations or commiserations should be offered all around. Such details may sound trifling but it is such traditions of the game that underpin the respectful manner in which cricket is played.

Sometime after each game the captain should revisit the score book to analyse the performance and form strategies for improving both the captain's and the team's performance. The captain should identify shortcomings within individual performances and identify remedial solutions and drills. For example, if a batter is struggling against a certain style of bowling, arrange the appropriate coaching and net practices to assist the batter and the team as a whole will benefit.

SYNOPSIS

The cricketer given the job of captain has been judged to hold the necessary personality and qualities to bring out the best in the side and should take a great deal of confidence and satisfaction from this fact alone.

However, concentrating on all the captain's duties as well as personally contributing to the team effort is not something all cricketers can manage. The weight of the captain's mantle has been known to lead to a sharp drop in form for the elected individual. To avoid taking on too much the captain should ask for help and share the considerable load by delegating some of the duties to the more experienced and capable team members. Involving players to assist in areas such as organizing the warm-up will not only reduce the burden on the captain but will also serve to bond the team together.

The captain should also make the conscious decision and take the necessary time to enjoy their cricket and their position at the heart of the side.

10 THINGS TO REMEMBER

1 All developing cricketers will improve by better understanding the captain's various responsibilities, considerations and potential strategies.

2 The captain of a cricket team bears the overall responsibility for both the team's successes and failures.

3 Selecting a balanced team will provide the necessary resources to implement changes in strategy that may be required as the game develops.

4 A player with slightly less skill than another but with a significantly better attitude will always prove to be the greater asset.

5 The captain should be well prepared ahead of a fixture both practically and with a suitable game plan.

6 To avoid injuries, a team warm-up should be planned ahead of each innings.

7 A good captain leads by example. Their personal performance should reflect the attitude, discipline and all of the standards expected of the team. The captain is also duty bound to ensure that all play is conducted within the Spirit of the Game as well as within the Laws.

8 Captains should neither ask a cricketer to field closer to the bat than the player is comfortable with nor without the necessary protective equipment.

9 In situations when the game plan is not working, the strategy should be changed immediately.

10 The best captains remember to enjoy their position at the heart of their cricket team.

7

··

Training for cricket

In this chapter you will learn:
• *the importance of fitness*
• *the importance of good nutrition*
• *the importance of practising.*

Sports science

Cricket is a physically demanding sport and elevating levels of fitness undoubtedly improve a cricketer's all-round performance. This fact has been universally accepted and over recent years the professional ranks have demanded a new breed of athletic cricketer. Quicker in the field and when running between the wickets, fit cricketers also hold advantages including more power, better stamina, quicker recovery and are less likely to suffer from injuries.

ENERGY

Muscles are fuelled with energy from stored deposits of carbohydrates and fat. For low intensity endurance activities, such as the walking or the jogging a cricketer does while fielding, the energy the muscles require is produced in the body by using oxygen to burn both fat and carbohydrates. The process of producing energy by using oxygen to burn fat or carbohydrate is termed as 'aerobic energy production'.

When rapid increases in muscle activity occur and aerobic energy production is not sufficient, the extra energy required is produced by converting carbohydrates into lactic acid without using oxygen, i.e 'anaerobic'. The process of producing energy without using oxygen to burn carbohydrate is termed as 'anaerobic energy production'.

The lactic acid produced in the process is waste and has a fatiguing effect on the body.

Raising levels of fitness improves the body's ability to produce energy aerobically, thereby decreasing the production of lactic acid making the body more efficient when metabolizing carbohydrate.

Aerobic fitness can be developed with various forms of endurance exercise such as jogging, swimming or cycling. Improvements in aerobic fitness will increase your levels of stamina and cardiovascular endurance and, as a result, activities such as fielding, bowling longer spells or running between the wickets will feel less demanding.

Levels of anaerobic fitness can be improved through intensive exercises such as repetitive sprints which also help to improve strength and agility. Elevating your levels of anaerobic fitness will increase your speed and strength and therefore improve your effectiveness when batting, bowling and fielding.

Flexibility is also important to a cricketer and should be improved by following an appropriate stretching drill. Improving the body's flexibility will assist a cricketer's speed and agility.

The importance of warming up

A thorough warm-up should be performed before any cricket match or practice to prepare the body for the whole range of movements likely to be required in the sport and also to reduce the chance of injury. A proper warm-up raises mental awareness, improves coordination, improves the elasticity and contractibility of muscles and increases the efficiency of the respiratory and cardiovascular systems. An effective warm-up should last 20–30 minutes, start gradually and progressively increase in intensity.

Example pre-match warm-up

1 Commence with a pulse-raising activity such as a jog around the ground, progressive running drills or simple games such as hand hockey or bounce passing. Start at your own comfortable pace and gradually increase the intensity of your running. The aim is to gradually increase cardiovascular output and enhance blood flow to joints and muscles.

2 Introduce stretches such as pendulum hip swings, back rolls and lunge steps. These dynamic stretches should cover the calve muscles, working through the thighs and hips, and then stretch the trunk and back. Move up through your chest, shoulders and arms and finish with the neck muscles. Stretches should also be adapted by the player depending on their role within the team. Batters may concentrate on hamstrings and calves as well as quickening feet movement, bowlers may concentrate on stretching the trunk, lower back, shoulders and arms while wicket keepers concentrate on hamstrings, calves, groin and back flexibility as well as quickening sideways movement. Cold muscles should never be stretched.

3 Spend a further ten to 15 minutes engaged in a specific group fielding drill such as one-handed underarm pickup and throws, catching on the move or retrieving a ball and throwing it back to the wicket keeper. Finish with role specific technical activities; batters will practise in pairs with throw downs, bowlers will bowl to a catching mitt on the edge of the square and the wicket keeper will practise reaction improving close catching.

Keep your body warm during your match or practice by wearing warm clothing and by jogging and stretching in between overs.

The importance of cooling down

A thorough cool-down should be performed after any cricket match or practice to reduce muscle soreness and to help the body to recovery. A proper cool-down allows the heart, metabolic and respiratory rates to gradually return to normal and encourages the effective re-absorption of the extra blood and waste products that concentrate in the muscles after physical exercise. A cool-down should last 15–20 minutes and progressively decrease in intensity. A cool-down may consist of five minutes of gentle jogging followed by stretching all the major muscle groups. Cool-downs should incorporate similar dynamic stretch routines as in the warm-up. During your cool-down it is advisable to put on an extra layer or two of clothing to help preserve your muscle temperature.

Nutrition for cricketers

Healthy eating throughout the year should become an important part of your lifestyle. Good nutrition helps to maintain a cricketer's energy levels throughout a match, aids recovery in between matches and maintains general body functions.

A healthy or balanced diet for a cricketer should consist primarily of carbohydrates, the majority of which should be starch-based, for example, wholegrain breads and cereals, potatoes, pasta and rice. To ensure variety try to include other sources of carbohydrate, for example, fruit, jams, oat-type biscuits, etc. as well. Fat sources in the diet include cheese, margarine, olive oil, nuts, avocados and chocolate. Restrict fried or fatty foods based around animal products, for example, fatty meat, cream, takeaways, etc., as a high fat intake may lead to other health issues, in addition to promoting weight gain. Overweight cricketers tire more quickly and are more likely to suffer from stress-related injuries. Protein-containing foods include meat, poultry, eggs, legumes, tofu, Quorn, milk and cheese and a protein source should be included at each mealtime.

Cricketers must possess the necessary energy reserves to sustain their activities throughout the course of a match or practice. Meals high in starchy carbohydrates, for example, chicken and pasta, tuna sandwich, or beef stir-fry should be consumed two to three hours before every match or practice as this is the approximate time it takes for food to clear from the stomach. During matches/practice, healthy snacks, for example, sandwich, hot cross bun, banana, yoghurt, etc., and a drink of water or a sports drink containing carbohydrate (for energy) and salt (to speed up absorption) should be available and consumed as required. Snacks containing carbohydrates based around sugars, for example, jam tarts, jaffa cakes, fruit juices and jelly babies, can be used to provide the body with a rapid supply of energy but should not be consumed too frequently. Excess carbohydrate not used by the body is either stored in muscle or as fat.

Consume meals high in starchy carbohydrates (as above) within two hours of finishing all cricketing activities, as during this time the body can replace the carbohydrate stores used up in exercise more effectively.

FLUID INTAKE

It is not uncommon for an adult cricketer to lose between three and five litres of fluid during a match. Do not wait to become thirsty before replacing this lost fluid as dehydrating to any degree will adversely affect your performance. Regularly drink small quantities of fluid in order to stay hydrated when involved in any cricketing activity.

Alcohol acts as a diuretic and therefore drinking alcoholic beverages is not an effective way to replace lost fluids. However magnificent the victory or terrible the loss, either celebrating with too much alcohol or drowning your sorrows will only serve to both damage your performances over the following days and your health over time.

Coaching

Whenever possible your practice should involve a qualified cricket coach evaluating and developing your skills. Most regions have several cricket clubs offering free qualified coaching so the importance and value of joining a local cricket club cannot be overstated.

Practice

There is no cricketer in existence that has been able to reach the higher levels of the game on their natural abilities alone. In fact what is often described as a cricketer's 'natural ability' is no more or less than the result of their extended effort and the highest levels of commitment put into their personal practice sessions. The reality is that the Laras, the Flintoffs, the Tendulkars, the Gilchrists, the Warnes and the Muralitharans of the cricketing world have the right to become quite irritated when referred to as 'naturally gifted' as their countless hours of individual practice are, by definition, disregarded with the label.

Practise as much as possible. Most fielding, bowling and certain batting skills can be honed alone. All your cricket practice should have a considered purpose by aiming to develop the areas of your game that either you, your captain or your coach feel require immediate remedy or improvement. During your practice it is crucial to refer to and focus on the correct fundamental techniques of the particular skill you wish to refresh or progress. Rope in a partner to develop your sessions and set yourself achievable targets. 'I will catch ten consecutive rebounds before I move on from my close catching practice.'

As mentioned, focusing on the correct technique is key within your practice sessions but should be avoided when you are involved in a match. Whether batting, bowling or fielding, relax and allow your developed and practised ability to flow as during a match becoming distracted by and trying to rectify some newly identified technical aspect of your game will only hinder your immediate performance.

10 THINGS TO REMEMBER

1 Fit cricketers hold advantages, including more power, better stamina and quicker recovery, and are less likely to suffer from injuries.

2 Improving the body's flexibility will assist a cricketer's speed and agility as well as reducing the chance of injury.

3 A proper warm-up raises mental awareness, improves coordination, improves the elasticity and contractibility of muscles and increases the efficiency of the respiratory and cardiovascular systems.

4 A proper cool-down allows the heart, metabolic and respiratory rates to gradually return to normal and encourages the effective re-absorption of the extra blood and waste products that concentrate in the muscles after physical exercise.

5 Good nutrition throughout the year helps to maintain a cricketer's energy levels during a match, aids recovery in between matches and maintains general body functions.

6 When involved in any cricketing activity, regularly drink small quantities of fluid in order to stay hydrated.

7 Whenever possible your practice should involve a qualified cricket coach evaluating and developing your skills.

8 Set achievable goals within your practice sessions.

9 Always focus on the correct technique within your practice sessions.

10 During a game and whether batting, bowling or fielding, relax and allow your technique and ability to flow.

8

8

....

Umpiring

In this chapter you will learn:
- **the role of the umpire**
- **judging 'no-balls' and 'wides'**
- **how to interpret the LBW law.**

This chapter will provide an understanding of the role and the responsibilities of the umpires and help to demystify some of the thorny issues surrounding umpiring decision making but does not intend to provide a comprehensive guide to the interpretation and application of the Laws.

The role of the umpires

Club and school cricket matches require two umpires to control the game within the Laws and every cricketer will further round their own game by developing a practical knowledge of both the role of the umpires and the Laws of Cricket. The umpires must interpret these Laws with total impartiality, with consistency in their decision making and with the necessary confidence and authority to inspire respect from the cricketers. The Laws of Cricket are too lengthy to be included here but can either be viewed at or downloaded from the MCC website (www.lords.org/laws-and-spirit/).

The umpires stand in two specific positions on the field of play in order to observe the action and to best judge the decisions they must make during the course of the match. One umpire stands directly behind the stumps at the bowler's end (the non-striker's end) of the pitch while the other umpire takes up a position at the striker's end of the pitch, square of the batter and usually stands at the position of square leg. The umpire standing at the non-striker's end is responsible for judgements including LBW appeals, catches, run out appeals at the non-striker's end, no-balls, wides, byes and leg byes. The umpire standing at the striker's end looks directly down the line of the batter's popping crease and judges decisions including stumping appeals, hit wicket appeals, run out appeals at the striker's end and wicket keeping no-balls. The umpires rotate their respective positions at the end of every over of each innings.

The umpire standing at the non-striker's end must ascertain whether the bowler intends to bowl right handed or left handed, from over or around the wicket and relays this information to the batter. The batter will then usually ask for a guard (see page 39). The umpire stands directly behind the stumps and carefully guides the batter to their requested guard.

Both umpires need to count the deliveries of each over and the umpire at the bowler's end calls 'over' after six legitimate deliveries. Though counting the six 'fair' deliveries of each over may seem one of the simpler tasks of the umpires, so much can happen during an over that umpires either carry six small stones and register a fair delivery by passing a stone from one hand or pocket to the other or use a mechanical counter to keep an accurate record. Even with this assistance, umpires are often seen referring with each other or on occasion even with the scorers to clarify the number of fair deliveries bowled.

The umpires must check that each delivery is fair, i.e. not a no-ball or a wide and if the delivery is deemed a no-ball the umpire must call 'no-ball!' immediately and clearly. Batters should not be given out by the umpires when a no-ball has been bowled unless the batter has handled the ball, hit the ball twice, obstructed the field or more commonly been run out. (See page 165 for a definition of these rules.)

Insight

An early call of 'no-ball!' is facilitated by the umpire breathing in as the bowler approaches their delivery stride.

Judging 'no-balls'

According to the Laws the umpire standing at the non-striker's end judges a delivery to be a no-ball when:

1 In the delivery stride either the bowler's back foot lands outside or touches the return crease or the front foot lands without some

part of the foot, whether grounded or raised, behind the line of the popping crease.

2 A delivery either bounces more than twice or rolls along the ground before it reaches the popping crease.

3 Any delivery, other than a slow paced delivery, passes or would pass without bouncing above the batter's waist level when standing upright at the crease.

4 A slow paced delivery passes or would pass without bouncing above the batter's shoulder level when standing upright at the crease.

5 Any fielder, other than the bowler, touches or extends any part of the body over the pitch before the ball has made contact with the bat or batter or the ball has passed the bat.

The umpire standing at the striker's end judges a delivery to be a 'no-ball' when:

1 At the moment of the bowler's delivery, there are more than two fielders, other than the wicket keeper, positioned behind the line of the popping crease on the batter's leg side.

2 The wicket keeper does not remain wholly behind the wicket at the striker's end before the delivery either touches the bat or batter, the ball passes the wicket at the striker's end or the batter attempts to take a run.

A no-ball takes precedent over a wide delivery and, as such, a no-ball that is directed out of the reach of the batter is still called as a no-ball by the umpires and is not called as a wide.

Judging 'wide deliveries'

According to the Laws the umpire standing at the non-striker's end judges a delivery to be a wide delivery (a 'wide') unless the ball is within striking distance of the batter by means of a normal cricket stroke when the batter is standing in a normal position on the popping crease. The umpire should not call a delivery as being a wide if:

1 The ball touches either the bat or the batter.

2 The batter backs away from the line of the delivery and subsequently causes the ball to pass wide of their position.

3 The batter moves towards the delivery and resultantly brings the ball sufficiently within reach to be able to strike it with a normal cricket stroke.

The ten modes of dismissal

The umpires must watch each delivery and follow the subsequent action closely in order to judge when a batter should be given out. The umpires' hearing is also used to gather clues in order to attain an accurate overview of the ensuing action. The umpires look for visual clues such as the ball deviating when it passes the batter and audible clues to differentiate between a ball clipping the bat and a ball being deflected from some other part of the batter.

When the fielding side think they have dismissed a batter, a member of the fielding team must appeal by asking the umpire 'How's that?' or more than likely 'HOWZAAAAAT!!!'

There are ten different ways a batter can be given out:

1 Caught – The striking batter is caught out when the ball is caught and held by a member of the fielding side either directly from the bat or directly from a hand gripping the bat.
2 Bowled – The striking batter is bowled out when the wicket is broken with the bowler's delivery. A batter is bowled out whether or not the ball is touched or deflected into the stumps by the batter.
3 Leg before wicket (LBW) – see page 166.
4 Run out – Either batter is run out when the wicket is broken by a member of the fielding side and a batter's bat or foot is not properly grounded behind the line of the popping crease. Batters can be run out off a wide delivery or a no-ball.
5 Stumped – The striking batter is stumped when the wicket is broken by the wicket keeper and the batter's bat or foot is not properly grounded behind the line of the popping crease but is not attempting to run. A batter can be given out stumped off a wide delivery but not off a no-ball.
6 Hit wicket – The striking batter is given out hit wicket when dislodging his own bails during the period between the bowler entering his delivery stride and the moment after the batter sets off of to run – i.e. if the batter breaks his own wicket when preparing to receive a delivery, while receiving a delivery or when setting off for their first run, the striking batter will be given out hit wicket.
7 Handled the ball – Either batter is given out handled the ball for deliberately handling the ball while it is in play without

firstly gaining permission from the fielding side unless they are returning the ball to a fielder.

8 Double hit – The striking batter is given out for deliberately hitting the ball twice unless in the process of protecting his wicket by guarding the stumps.

9 Obstructing the field – Either batter can be given out for deliberately distracting (including by shouting) or preventing fielders from fielding or catching the ball.

10 Timed out – A batter is timed out when a new batter takes over three minutes (90 seconds in the T20 format) from the fall of the previous wicket to reach their appropriate position at the crease.

When an umpire is certain a wicket has been taken, they will indicate their decision by raising an index finger above the head in the direction of the dismissed batter. The Laws state that the benefit of any doubt in the umpire's mind must be given to the batter. So if in doubt, it's Not out.

THE LEG BEFORE WICKET (LBW) LAW

Just like the offside rule in football, cricket's LBW law has a reputation for being extraordinarily complex, but assuming the bowler has bowled a fair delivery, any LBW appeal can be judged against just four questions.

1 If the ball pitched before striking the batter, are you certain the ball pitched in line between both sets of stumps or on the off side?

2 Are you certain that the ball did not initially strike the bat or the hand holding the bat? A batter can be adjudged to be leg before wicket after being initially struck by the ball on any part of their body or equipment except the bat or a hand (including the glove) holding the bat.

3 Decide whether the batter made a genuine attempt to play the ball and if so, the question is whether the ball first struck the batter in line between both sets of stumps? If not, the question is whether the ball first struck the batter in line between both sets of stumps or on the off side of the stumps?

4 Are you certain the ball would have gone on to hit the stumps?

To give a batter out LBW the answer to each relevant question must be yes.

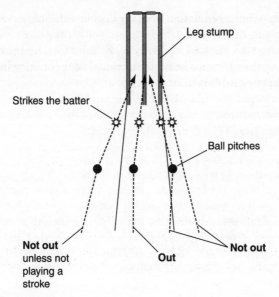

Leg stump

Strikes the batter

Ball pitches

Not out
unless not
playing a
stroke

Out

Not out

Figure 8.1 How to decide an LBW.

When considering whether the ball is certain to go on to hit the stumps the umpire will contemplate how far the ball has left to travel after striking the batter. A batter playing a front foot shot may be struck by the ball over two metres in front of the stumps and the judgement of whether the delivery would have gone on to hit the stumps is a far more difficult one than when a batter is struck on the back leg right in front of the stumps.

The flight of the delivery will guide the umpire's decision as to whether the ball would bounce over the stumps or not. The umpire must consider whether the delivery was rising or falling when it hit the batter and how high up the batter the initial contact was. Remember that if any doubt the umpire has to give a favourable decision to the batter.

Byes and leg byes

If a fair delivery passes the batter without touching the bat or batter and, for example, is also missed by the wicket keeper, any runs completed are referred to as 'byes' and are signalled as such by the umpires.

If a fair delivery misses the bat or a hand holding the bat, but touches any other part of the batter's body or equipment, any runs completed by the batters are signalled as 'leg byes'. In order for a leg bye to be awarded the umpire must be of the opinion that the striking batter either attempted to play a shot or tried to avoid being struck by the ball.

Penalty runs

The most common example of penalty runs being awarded is when the ball hits an unused helmet left by the fielding side directly behind the wicket keeper and the batting side are automatically awarded five penalty runs. Five penalty runs are also occasionally awarded to batting or fielding teams when the umpires are certain that unfair play has been observed. Unfair play covers abuses of the Laws such as ball tampering, a batter deliberately running a short run or a fielder deliberately obstructing a batter.

The protected area

The protected area of the wicket is an imaginary rectangle that covers the area of the pitch that the bowlers need to avoid when following through after bowling a delivery. The area is protected by the umpires because bowlers' footsteps create rough patches around the crease which can cause the ball to bounce and turn unpredictably. These areas can be exploited by other bowlers and especially by the spinners. If bowlers were permitted to follow through and routinely run onto this protected area, rough patches would quickly be created in line with the stumps which would give an unfair advantage to the bowlers.

The protected area is usually indicated by two horizontal markings five feet from the popping crease on either side of the pitch. This gives the umpires an indication of the area the bowler must avoid when following through.

When a bowler runs onto the protected area they will be given a warning by the umpire standing at the non-striker's end of the pitch, who then informs the other umpire, the captain of the fielding side and both batters that the bowler has been cautioned. If the same bowler runs onto the protected area for a second time in an innings, then the umpire will issue a second warning in exactly the same manner as the first. If the bowler runs onto the protected area for a third time, the umpire will instruct the captain of the fielding side to remove the bowler from the attack immediately. That bowler will not be permitted to bowl for the rest of the innings.

Umpiring signals

The umpires indicate their decisions to the scorers with the following signals:

Figure 8.2 **Dead ball:** *crossing and re-crossing the wrists below the waist.*

Figure 8.3 **No-ball:** *extending one arm horizontally.*

Figure 8.4 **Out:** *raising an index finger above the head.*

Figure 8.5 **Wide:** *extending both arms horizontally.*

Figure 8.6 **Boundary 4:** *waving an arm from side to side, finishing with the arm held across the chest.*

Figure 8.7 **Boundary 6:** *raising both arms above the head.*

Figure 8.8 **Bye:** *raising an open hand above the head.*

Figure 8.9 **Leg bye:** *touching a raised knee with the hand.*

Figure 8.10 **Five penalty runs awarded to the batting side:** *repeatedly tapping one shoulder with the opposite hand.*

Figure 8.11 **Five penalty runs awarded to the fielding side:** *placing one hand on the opposite shoulder.*

Figure 8.12 **New ball:** *holding the new ball above the head.*

Figure 8.13 **Short run:** *bending one arm upwards and touching the nearer shoulder with the fingers.*

Figure 8.14 **Commencement of last hour:** *pointing to a raised wrist with the other hand.*

Figure 8.15 **Revoke last signal:** *touching both shoulders, each with the opposite hand.*

All umpire's signals need to be acknowledged by the scorers before play is re-commenced.

Just like the cricketers around them, all umpires will make mistakes from time to time and familiarizing yourself with the umpire's numerous responsibilities will hopefully assist you to understand just how difficult the role can be and help you to cope with the disappointment of being the subject of a bad umpiring decision. An essential aspect of the personal test of character the sport of cricket provides is in developing enough discipline and mental toughness to suffer outrageous fortune without complaint.

5 THINGS TO REMEMBER

1 Club and school cricket matches require two umpires.

2 Umpires are expected to interpret the Laws with impartiality and with consistency in their decision making.

3 The umpires must count and check that each delivery is fair, closely scrutinize the subsequent action, then communicate their decisions with clear calls and signals.

4 There are ten different ways a batter can be given out.

5 The benefit of any doubt must be given to the batter. So if in doubt, it's 'Not out'.

9

Scoring

In this chapter you will learn:
- *how to score to an internationally recognized standard*
- *how to interpret a cricketer's statistics.*

Learning to score is made a considerably simpler task with a match to watch during the process. Learning to score while at a ground, in front of the television or even by scoring a game generated by a games console can mean that the process of understanding the basics of scoring is achievable within an hour or so.

The role of the scorers

The Laws state that cricket matches require two scorers. Scorers are required to record the runs scored, the wickets taken and the overs bowled. This is the bare minimum of information required by the Laws but in reality scorers generally record a great many more details of the game.

Scorers accept and acknowledge every signal the umpires make even when a particular signal is thought by the scorer to be incorrect. The scorers accurately and clearly record these events in the score book. It is not within a scorer's jurisdiction to correct the umpires' signals however misguided or illogical the decision might appear. The score book creates an invaluable source of information for players and officials alike.

By consistently using the following internationally recognized symbols and system of scoring, any experienced scorer will be able to take over the scoring of an innings without significantly altering the style and readability of the score book.

Scoring symbols

Numbers are used to denote runs scored by a batter and symbols are used to signify **extras**.

Fair delivery and no runs scored 'dot ball'	•
Fair delivery and the striking batter scores runs	**1 2 3** etc.
No-ball with no other runs scored	○
No-ball and the striking batter scores runs	① ② ③ etc.
No-ball and the batters run without hitting the ball	⊙ ⊙ ⊙ etc.
Wide ball with no other runs scored	+
Wide ball and batters run	+ + + etc.
Byes	△ △ △ etc.
Leg byes	▽ ▽ ▽ etc.
Bowler credited with a wicket	**W**
Wide ball and the bowler credited with a wicket (stumping)	**W**+

Underlining a symbol or number signifies that the batters are at the opposite ends of the pitch than would be expected, for example, the correct entry in the score book would be <u>1</u> if the batters ran two runs but the umpire has signalled that one run was not properly completed. The same principle applies if the batters crossed before the striking batter is caught out and the correct entry in the score book would be <u>W</u>.

The score book

Most of the details within the header are recorded by the scorers before the start of an innings.

North Maidenhead C.C. vs. Berkstown C.C.
Venue: *Summerleaze Ground*   Date: *25th April, 2010*
Weather: *Hot and sunny*
Innings of: *North Maidenhead*   Toss won by: *Berkstown*
Type of match: *40 Over*   Start: *12 pm*   Finish: *3.05 pm*

Each delivery is initially recorded in the **bowling analysis** (see Figure 9.1), then recorded in the **batting section** and then any runs scored added to the **cumulative run tally**. Any other important incident (for example, the time a fielder left and returned to the field) should be recorded in the **notes** box.

Figure 9.1 The bowling analysis.

Bowler	1	2	3	4	5	6	7	8	WD	NB	Balls	Overs	Mdns	Runs	Wkts	Avg
1 D. BAIG	6 - 0	10 - 0	13 - 0	19 - 0	28 - 0	33 - 1	37 - 1	42 - 1			48	8	0	42	1	42
2 K. FALK	3 - 0	7 - 0	10 - 1	16 - 1	17 - 1	17 - 1	19 - 3	25 - 3	1	11	51	8	1	25	3	8.3
3 B. WIGLEY	11 - 0	13 - 0	14 - 1	19 - 1	24 - 1	26 - 1	38 - 1	42 - 1			48	8	0	42	1	42
4 G. SANGHA	3 - 0	14 - 0	23 - 0	29 - 0	33 - 1	42 - 1	50 - 1	61 - 1			48	8	0	61	1	61
5 R. McNAMARA	2 - 0	10 - 0	14 - 0	19 - 0							24	4	0	19	0	–
6 D. SIMPSON	10 - 1	20 - 1	23 - 2	32 - 2							24	4	0	32	2	16

	WD	NB	Balls	Overs	Mdns	Runs	Wkts
Bowling totals	1	2	243	40	1	221	8
Fielding extras & other dismissals						8	1
Provisional score						229	9
Penalties in other innings							
Final score							

In the bowling analysis each box represents one over bowled by a bowler. Each over is denoted by two rows of three symbols with any extra deliveries placed in a row in between. The rows of three can be arranged vertically or horizontally but either method should be consistently employed throughout a score book and must not be changed during a match. For example, the six deliveries of D. Baig's first over (shown in Figure 9.1) have been recorded as:

• 2 • • • 4	▶ Ball 1 – fair delivery and no score ▶ Ball 2 – fair delivery and two runs scored by the batter ▶ Ball 3 – fair delivery and no score ▶ Ball 4 – fair delivery and no score ▶ Ball 5 – fair delivery and no score ▶ Ball 6 – fair delivery and four runs scored by the batter

The seven deliveries of K. Falk's fourth over have been recorded as:

• 4 • • • ①	▶ Ball 1 – fair delivery and no score ▶ Ball 2 – fair delivery and four runs scored by the batter ▶ Ball 3 – fair delivery and no score ▶ Ball 4 – fair delivery and no score ▶ Ball 5 – fair delivery and no score ▶ Ball 6 – 'no-ball' called with the batter striking the ball and running one run (one no-ball and one run) ▶ Ball 7 – fair delivery and no score

M	The six dots of a **maiden** over (an over in which no runs are conceded by the bowler) are joined together to form a capital letter M. A capital letter W is formed when a bowler is credited with a wicket during a maiden over. To ensure the record is readable, the symbols of wickets, byes and leg byes should not be struck through by the M or W.
W	
W 4 • 2 2 2 10 – 1	At the end of each over a running total of the bowler's runs conceded and wickets taken are recorded in the bottom section of the box.

Totals	
WD	NB
1	*11*

Using only the figure 1, occurrences of no-balls and wides are recorded in the bowler's **totals** column. Any runs scored from no-balls or wides are added to the **extras** section in the batting section and not in the **totals** column.

The end of a bowler's spell is marked with a vertical line.

THE BATTING SECTION

The batting section (see Figure 9.2) records all runs scored and contains the details of each batter's innings and dismissal.

A symbol is added for every delivery faced which should mirror the corresponding delivery in the bowling analysis. When a batter is dismissed their innings is closed with two slashes, the details of the dismissal recorded in the 'How out' column and where applicable the bowler credited with the wicket. When a batter is not out or is dismissed in a manner not credited to the bowler, the manner of dismissal is recorded only in the 'How out' column using the mode of dismissal (often abbreviated) and the name of any fielder involved. For example, in Figure 9.2, M. Malik was caught out by J. Lloyd and the bowler was K. Falk.

Keeping track of and totting up an individual batter's innings is made quicker and easier by inserting a slash and noting the batter's score after each ten deliveries faced.

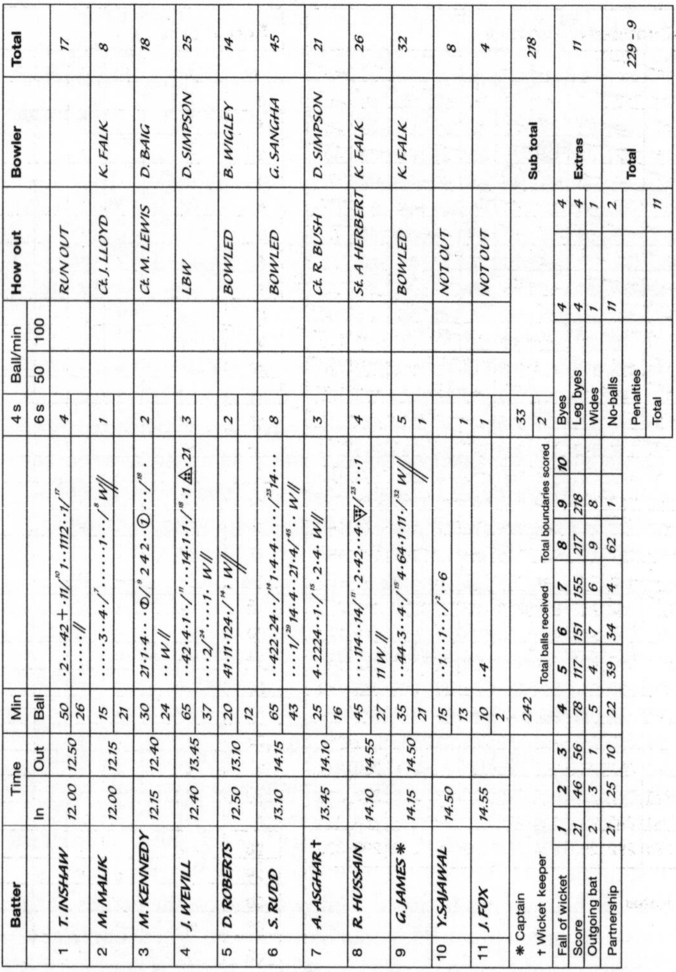

Figure 9.2 The batting section.

#	Batter	In	Out	Min	Ball	Scoring	4 s	6 s	How out	Bowler	Total
1	T. INSHAW	12.00	12.50	50	26	.2-..42+.111/¹⁰.1-.1112-.1/¹⁷ ......//	4		RUN OUT		17
2	M. MALIK	12.00	12.15	15	21	.....3-.4-/.......1-..1/⁸ W//	1		Ct. J. LLOYD	K. FALK	8
3	M. KENNEDY	12.15	12.40	30	24	21-1-4-.Φ/⁹ 2 4 2-.①-...¹⁸. .. W//	2		Ct. M. LEWIS	D. BAIG	18
4	J. WEVILL	12.40	13.45	65	37	.42-4-1-./¹¹.1 4-1-1-/⁴⁸.1△.21 ...2/²⁴....1-. W//	3		LBW	D. SIMPSON	25
5	D. ROBERTS	12.50	13.10	20	12	41-11-124-/¹⁴. W///	2		BOWLED	B. WIGLEY	14
6	S. RUDD	13.10	14.15	65	43	.-422-24-./¹⁴ 1-4-4-...../²³ 14-..-/ .....1/²⁹ 14-4-.21-4/⁴⁶-. W//	8		BOWLED	G. SANGHA	45
7	A. ASGHAR †	13.45	14.10	25	16	4-2224-1-/¹¹.2-4- W//	3		Ct. R. BUSH	D. SIMPSON	21
8	R. HUSSAIN	14.10	14.55	45	27	..114-14/¹¹.2-42-4-W/²³...1 11 W//	4		St. A HERBERT	K. FALK	26
9	G. JAMES *	14.15	14.50	35	21	.44-3-.4-/¹⁴ 4-64-1-11-/¹² W/ ///	5	1	BOWLED	K. FALK	32
10	Y. SAJAWAL	14.50		15	13	.1-.1-./³.-6	1		NOT OUT		8
11	J. FOX	14.55		10	2	.4	1		NOT OUT		4
	* Captain				242		33	2		Sub total	218
	† Wicket keeper									Extras	11
										Total	229 - 9

Extras:

Byes	4	4
Leg byes	4	4
Wides	1	1
No-balls	2	2
Penalties		
Total	11	11

Fall of wicket	1	2	3	4	5	6	7	8	9	10
Score	21	46	56	78	117	151	155	217	218	
Outgoing bat	2	3	1	5	4	7	6	9	8	
Partnership	21	25	10	22	39	34	4	62	1	

Total balls received

Total boundaries scored

No-balls, byes and leg byes are counted as deliveries faced by the batter but though not credited to the batter, they should also be

178

Cumulative run tally

1	2	3	4	5	6	7	8	9	10
11	12	13	14	15	16	17	18	19	20
21	22	23	24	25	26	27	28	29	30
31	32	33	34	35	36	37	38	39	40
41	42	43	44	45	46	47	48	49	50
51	52	53	54	55	56	57	58	59	60
61	62	63	64	65	66	67	68	69	70
71	72	73	74	75	76	77	78	79	80
81	82	83	84	85	86	87	88	89	90
91	92	93	94	95	96	97	98	99	100
101	102	103	104	105	106	107	108	109	110
111	112	113	114	115	116	117	118	119	120
121	122	123	124	125	126	127	128	129	130
131	132	133	134	135	136	137	138	139	140
141	142	143	144	145	146	147	148	149	150
151	152	153	154	155	156	157	158	159	160
161	162	163	164	165	166	167	168	169	170
171	172	173	174	175	176	177	178	179	180
181	182	183	184	185	186	187	188	189	190
191	192	193	194	195	196	197	198	199	200
201	202	203	204	205	206	207	208	209	210
211	212	213	214	215	216	217	218	219	220
221	222	223	224	225	226	227	228	229	230
231	232	233	234	235	236	237	238	239	240
241	242	243	244	245	246	247	248	249	250
251	252	253	254	255	256	257	258	259	260
261	262	263	264	265	266	267	268	269	270
271	272	273	274	275	276	277	278	279	280
281	282	283	284	285	286	287	288	289	290
291	292	293	294	295	296	297	298	299	300

Notes

End of over pen

Ov	Runs	W	B	B	F
0	0				
1	6		1		
2	9		2		
3	13		1		
4	17		2		
5	20		1		
6	23	1	2		
7	29	1	1		
8	35	1	2		
9	44	1	1		
10	45	1	2		
11	50	2	1		
12	50	2	2		
13	61	3	3		
14	64	3	4		
15	66	3	3		
16	77	3	4		
17	78	4	3		
18	87	4	4		
19	95	4	3		
20	98	4	5		
21	103	4	3		
22	111	4	5		
23	113	4	3		
24	117	4	5		
25	127	5	6		
26	132	5	5		
27	142	5	6		
28	148	5	4		
29	151	6	6		
30	155	7	4		
31	164	7	6		
32	173	7	4		
33	185	7	3		
34	193	7	4		
35	201	7	3		
36	212	7	4		
37	216	7	1		
38	218	9	2		
39	223	9	1		
40	229	9	2		

Figure 9.3 A cumulative run tally.

denoted in the batting section to help maintain an accurate record. For example, the tenth delivery faced by M. Kennedy was a no-ball. Kennedy (see Figure 9.2) struck the ball and ran one run. The no-ball is recorded in the batting section and the extras section and, in addition, Kennedy has one run added to his score.

At the fall of each wicket, the score, the number of the dismissed batter and the partnership are recorded in the 'Fall of wicket' section.

During play the running total is maintained by filling in the **cumulative run tally**.

The numbers within the grid are crossed off as runs are scored. Single runs are crossed off with a diagonal line within a box and multiple scores recorded with a continuous line across the appropriate number of boxes.

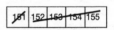

To indicate a score that continues into a second line, the line is extended beyond the grid on the first line and re-started before the grid on the second line.

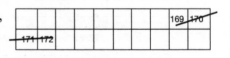

Denoting runs scored as extras in this section helps maintain an accurate record.

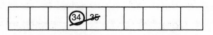

For example, the thirty-fourth run was a no-ball and the batters also ran one (the thirty-fifth run); the circle in the cumulative run tally denotes the no-ball and both runs are crossed off the tally.

At the end of each over, a row in the 'End of over' section is completed. The score, the total number of wickets, the number of the bowler (taken from the bowling analysis) and any incidents of penalty runs awarded to

End of over				Pen	
Ov	Runs	W	B	B	F
0	0				
1	6		1		

the batting or fielding sides are recorded (always entering the figure 1 for each incident of penalty runs being awarded).

Any penalty runs awarded to the side batting second are recorded in over number '0'.

Scorers should check the accuracy of their record at the end of every over and also during all other opportune breaks in play. This ensures that errors are quickly identified and can be promptly rectified.

At the end of each innings, in the batting section the scorer must:

1 Record 'Not out' in the 'How out' box of any not out batter.
2 Record 'Retired not out' or 'Retired out' in the 'How out' box of any retired batter.
3 Any remaining batters should have 'DNB' (did not bat) recorded in their 'How out' box.
4 Total the runs scored by the batters and record in the 'Sub Total' box.
5 Total the no-balls, wides, byes, leg byes with any penalties and record in the 'Extras' box.
6 Add the batting total to the extras total and record in the 'Total' box with the total number of wickets taken.

Sub total	218
Extras	11
Total	229–9

7 Indicate in the record the batting side's captain and wicket keeper.

Then in the bowling analysis the scorer must:

1 Complete the bowling summary by recording the total number of **balls** bowled (including no-balls and wides), the total number of **overs** bowled, the total number of **maidens** bowled, the total number of **runs** conceded and the total number of **wickets** taken by each bowler.

2 Calculate the **average** for each bowler. This bowling average is calculated by dividing the runs conceded by the bowler by the wickets taken. When no wickets are taken a dash (–) is entered.

Totals		Balls	Overs	Mdns	Runs	Wkts	Avg
WD	NB						
0	0	48	8	0	42	1	42

3 Record the sum of these totals in the corresponding bowling totals boxes.

4 Record the runs and any wickets not attributed to the bowlers (one run out, four byes and four leg byes) in the 'Fielding extras and other dismissals' box.

5 Add these fielding extras and dismissals to the bowlers' wickets and runs and record in 'Provisional score' box (229–9).

Bowling totals		*1*	*2*	*243*	*40*	*1*	*221*	*8*
Fielding extras & other dismissals							*8*	*1*
Provisional score							*229*	*9*

PENALTY RUNS

When penalty runs are awarded to the batting side they are recorded in the 'End of Over' section (always entering the figure 1 for each incident of penalty runs being awarded) and also as fielding extras in the 'Extras' section.

When penalty runs are awarded to the fielding side they are recorded in the 'End of Over' section (always entering the figure 1 for each penalty awarded) and added to the fielding side's batting score. If the fielding side has already batted then the penalty runs are added to their provisional score. If the fielding side are yet to bat then any penalty runs will be added at the beginning of their innings.

Scorers can be assisted in their accuracy by remembering these 'three Cs':

Conciseness: Keep figures small and neat or you may not get everything in.

Concentration: It is imperative to keep your mind on the job of scoring.

Cross-checks: Whenever there is a moment to spare, batters' totals should be added to all extras and runs conceded by bowlers added to byes and leg byes and the two totals should be the same as one another and the cumulative total. This way any errors can be found early on.

Cricket statistics

The accurate maintaining of records throughout a season and career allows cricketers to measure their personal success with an array of statistics. Batting and bowling statistics can be compiled for any period of time but usually reflect a single season or a career.

BATTING STATISTICS

Batting statistics can be compiled for any period of time or any particular collection of matches (for example, 2007 Sunday League statistics) but usually reflect either a batter's single season or a career. Batting statistics include the following information:

I	NO	R	HS	Ave	BF	SR	100	50
131	7	4288	173*	34.58	10005	42.85	8	23

(* denotes not out)

▶ Innings (I): The number of innings in which the batter actually batted.
▶ Not outs (NO): The number of times the batter is not out at the conclusion of an innings they batted in.
▶ Runs (R): The total number of runs scored by the batter.
▶ High score (HS): The highest score ever made by the batter.
▶ Batting average (Ave): The total number of runs divided by the total number of innings in which the batter was out. The average number of runs a batter scores is considered the primary measure of an individual player's skill as a batter. A batting average can also be simply interpreted as being the approximate average number of runs the batter scores per innings.
▶ Balls faced (BF): The total number of balls received by batter, including no-balls but not including wides.
▶ Strike rate (SR): The number of runs scored per 100 balls faced. (Ten runs off 20 balls equates to a strike rate of 50.) The strike rate measures the effectiveness of each batter. The higher the strike rate, the more effective a batter is at scoring quickly. Given players of similar batting averages, the cricketer with the higher strike rate would be considered the better batter.
▶ Centuries (100): The number of innings in which the batter scored 100 runs or more.
▶ Half-centuries (50): The number of innings in which the batter scored 50 to 99 runs (centuries do not count as half-centuries as well).

BOWLING STATISTICS

Bowling statistics can be compiled for any period of time or any particular collection of matches but usually reflect either a bowler's single season or a career. Bowling statistics include the following information:

B	R	W	BB	Ave	Econ	SR	5W	10W
901	541	15	4/42	36.06	3.60	60.06	0	0

▶ Balls (B): The total number of balls bowled.
▶ Runs (R): The total number of runs conceded.
▶ Wickets (W): The total number of wickets taken.
▶ Best bowling (BB): The bowler's best bowling performance in a single innings is measured firstly by the greatest number of wickets taken in a single innings and secondly by the fewest runs conceded for that number of wickets.
▶ Bowling average (Ave): A bowler's bowling average is defined as the total number of runs conceded by the bowler divided by the number of wickets taken by the bowler, so the lower the average the better the bowler.
▶ Economy rate (Econ): The average number of runs conceded per over.
▶ Strike rate (SR): The average number of balls bowled per wicket taken (a strike rate of 48 means a bowler takes a wicket every 8 overs). Bowling strike rate is a measure of how frequently a bowler takes their wickets. The lower the strike rate, the more effective a bowler is considered.
▶ Five wickets in an innings (5w): The number of innings in which the bowler took at least five wickets.
▶ Ten wickets in a match (10w): The number of matches in which the bowler took at least ten wickets.

BOWLING ANALYSIS

The bowling analysis is a notation consisting of an individual bowler's overs bowled, maidens bowled, runs conceded and wickets taken (in that order), usually for a single innings but the bowling analysis can also be used to represent other time periods.

An analysis of 12–3–38–3 would indicate that a cricketer bowled 12 overs, of which three were maidens, conceded 38 runs and took three wickets.

5 THINGS TO REMEMBER

1 Club and school cricket matches require two scorers.

2 Scorers are required to record, as a minimum: the runs scored, the wickets taken and the overs bowled.

3 It is not within a scorer's jurisdiction to correct the umpires' signals.

4 Numbers are used to denote runs scored by a batter and symbols are used to signify extras.

5 Remember the 'three Cs': conciseness, concentration and cross-checks.

Equipment

In this chapter you will learn:
• *about the equipment required to play cricket*.

The cricket ball

A cricket ball is constructed of a cork core tightly wound in twine and covered with a leather case. The cover is stitched together forming a slightly raised seam around the ball's equator.

Traditionally the ball is dyed red but white balls have been introduced into certain fixtures to improve the ball's visibility against coloured clothing and under floodlights. Once dyed the ball is lacquered and polished.

Figure 10.1 A new cricket ball.

A cricket ball is designed to be used for an extended period of play and after repeated collisions with the ground, being struck by the batters and rolling across the playing area, the ball softens, the surface wears and the seam may become flattened. This deterioration in condition greatly influences the aerodynamic and dynamic properties of a cricket ball and consequently both the ball's movement in the air and bounce from the pitch become affected. A bowler's ability to harness these properties and the batter's ability to deal with the results is the measure of their individual talents.

The fielding side are permitted to polish the ball to help preserve its condition but spit and sweat are the only substances that can be applied to the ball to assist in this polishing. Applying any other substance to the ball, picking at the seam or deliberately scratching the ball are all considered ball tampering and against the Laws of Cricket and the Spirit of the Game. Polishing just one side of the ball and allowing the other side to deteriorate naturally can cause the ball to swerve in the air and therefore make the trajectory of the delivery more difficult to predict for the batters. This is why the fielding side are regularly seen rubbing one side of the ball on their trousers.

Insight

Due to their construction cricket balls are dense, hard and when travelling at speed can inflict serious injuries. When batting, keeping wicket or positioned as a close fielder make sure you wear the appropriate protective equipment.

Cricket bats

Almost any old bat will do.

Sir Don Bradman

There are many styles of cricket bat manufactured in a range of different sizes, weights and handle lengths but you need only really consider whether you have a bat that is the right size and weight for you.

Figure 10.2 Cricket bats.

The correct method to finding the right sized bat is simply by standing a bat upright next to you. The top of the handle should reach the bottom of your thigh pocket.

Weights of bats also vary and the correct method to see whether the weight of the bat is right for you is to grip the bat with only your top hand. If with just your top hand you can perform a controlled backswing and then comfortably perform both vertical and horizontal batting strokes, then that's the perfect weight bat for you.

A bat that is too big or heavy for a player will limit their ability to successfully play a wide range of shots. This is particularly critical for young players taking up cricket for the first time.

Footwear

Figure 10.3 Studded shoes are essential for soft ground, but pimpled soles are better for very hard ground.

With all the running, jumping and turning that cricketers are required to perform, the two most important qualities to look for in a cricket boot or shoe are comfort and grip. Shoes or boots with fitted studs are essential for grip when playing on soft ground, while pimpled rubber soles provide better grip on very hard ground. 'Half-spikes' refer to shoes or boots with a combination of both studs and pimples and are available for specialist batters who prefer shoes with studs for grip at the front of the sole and pimpled heels to facilitate their pivoting when playing certain batting strokes. Bowlers require plenty of grip and so usually prefer shoes or boots with studs fitted at both the front and back sections of the sole. Bowlers may also prefer the extra support around the ankle that bowling boots offer.

When purchasing your cricketing footwear, remember that you
may be wearing thick sports socks during cricketing activities and
your feet are certain to swell. Buy footwear half a size bigger than
fit comfortably in the shop.

Protective equipment

A cricket ball can cause injuries so wearing specialist protective
equipment is as essential as putting on your footwear and carrying a
bat. All schools and most cricket clubs can provide you with all the
protective equipment required to play cricket.

BATTING GLOVES

It is important that your hands and fingers are well protected when
you are batting. Each finger of both gloves has padded areas designed
to be flexible and therefore make it easy to hold the glove around
the bat handle. When gripping the bat correctly it is the thumb of
the bottom hand that is held lowest, in front and nearest the face
of the bat and therefore all batting gloves have extra protection on
the thumb of the bottom hand.

Figure 10.4 Batting gloves provide protection for your hands.

BATTING PADS

Make sure your batting pads fit comfortably and properly. The horizontal panels on the front of the pad (the knee-roll) should be exactly at knee level with the top section of the pads protecting the lower thighs. Batting pads that are too small or too big will restrict the movement in your knees and in turn hinder your stroke play and slow down your running between the wickets.

Figure 10.5 Make sure your batting pads fit properly.

HELMET

Wearing a helmet is compulsory for children under the age of 18 when batting, when standing up to the stumps as a wicket keeper and when positioned within 5.5 metres of the striking batter as a close fielder.

Though not compulsory for adult cricketers, the protection a helmet will afford the face and head makes the wearing of a helmet a very sensible practice for all cricketers when batting, when standing up to the stumps as a wicket keeper or when fielding very close to the batter.

Your helmet should be light, comfortable and conform to the highest possible safety standards. A good helmet will be impact resistant, constructed of a lightweight material and fully lined for increased shock absorption. The helmet should also be ventilated for improved air flow and come complete with a fully adjustable faceguard. Ensure the faceguard is properly adjusted so the ball cannot pass between the grill and the peak of the helmet.

Figure 10.6 A helmet provides essential protection for the face and head.

BOX

A protective box or cup (politely referred to as an abdominal guard) should always be worn to protect the groin area when either batting, keeping wicket or fielding in positions close to the batter.

WICKET KEEPING EQUIPMENT

The wicket keeper has the advantage of wearing specialist wicket keeping gloves which have extra protection around the ends of each finger and a web between the thumb and first finger to help catch the ball. Most wicket keepers also prefer to wear a pair of chamois or cotton inners underneath the main gloves for comfort. A wicket keeper also needs the extra protection of wearing a box and pads.

Wicket keeping pads are shorter and lighter in weight than batting pads making them easier and more comfortable for the wicket keeper to crouch, move and dive around in.

Figure 10.7 Specialist wicket keeping glove and pad.

OTHER PROTECTION

When batting, it is entirely up to the individual whether they wear an outer or inner thigh pad, an arm guard or chest guard. Outer thigh guards are recommended, as the front thigh is particularly vulnerable to being struck when a batter is getting into line properly.

Having access to the proper equipment will enhance your ability to develop the correct techniques. This can only serve to magnify your enjoyment of the greatest game on earth.

5 THINGS TO REMEMBER

1 When batting, keeping wicket or positioned as a close fielder, make sure you wear the appropriate protective equipment.

2 The right size and weight bat should reach the bottom of your thigh pocket and be light enough so that you can control its movements with just your top hand.

3 Your footwear should be comfortable and provide good grip.

4 Make sure your batting pads fit well. Pads that are too small or too big will hinder your stroke play and slow down your running between the wickets.

5 Wearing a helmet is compulsory for children under the age of 18 when batting, when standing up to the stumps as a wicket keeper and when positioned within 5.5 metres of the striking batter as a close fielder.

Glossary

This section should help you unravel the customized language and jargon employed to describe cricket. Some terms such as googly and off spin are not included as they are clearly described in previous chapters.

all out A side is all out when ten of the 11 batters are dismissed or retired.

appeal A member of the fielding side must appeal to the umpire when they think they have dismissed a batter ("Howzat!").

bat pad Another name for the fielding position short leg, placed to catch the ball ricocheting from the edge of the bat onto the pad.

beamer A delivery that does not bounce and is directed at the batter's head. A beamer is usually bowled accidentally and is considered to be an unfair and dangerous delivery.

beaten When a batter plays a stroke but fails to make contact with the ball, the batter is said to have been beaten either by the pace, the flight or the skill of the delivery.

block hole The area on the popping crease where the batter marks his guard. A delivery 'in the block hole' is intended to slip under the bat.

bowled out A batter is bowled out when their wicket is broken by the bowler's delivery whether or not the ball was touched by the batter or deflected into the stumps; a side is bowled out when ten of the 11 batters are dismissed or retired.

break the wicket The wicket may be considered broken (or 'put down') when at least one bail has been completely dislodged from the stumps by the ball, the batter, the bat or a fielder's hand holding the ball. If both bails have already been dislodged, to break the wicket a member of the fielding side must pull a stump from the ground with the hand or hands holding the ball.

bump ball An apparent catch that is not out because the ball has, in reality, been hit into the ground and then bounced into the fielder's grasp.

bye An extra run scored from a delivery that has not been touched by the bat or some part of the batter.

carry your bat When an opening batter remains not out when the rest of their team are bowled out.

caught behind Caught out by the wicket keeper.

charge A batter charges the bowler by moving attackingly down the pitch towards the delivery.

chuck To throw the ball instead of bowling the ball fairly. To bowl the ball fairly the bowler's elbow must not visibly straighten during the delivery action.

clean bowled When a batter completely misses the ball and is bowled out by the delivery.

closing the face Angling the bat face inwards in order to direct the delivery towards the leg side.

collapse When a batting side loses several wickets over a short period of time.

corridor of uncertainty The channel just outside off stump where the batter has a tricky decision whether to leave or play at the delivery.

cow corner Another name for the area of deep mid wicket.

crease The areas around the stumps marked with white lines.

cross bat shot When the bat is swung horizontally across the line of the delivery.

dolly A simple catch that lobs gently to a fielder.

dot ball A fair delivery from which no runs are scored and recorded in the score book with a dot.

duck An individual batting score of nought.

edge The outer sides of the bat and bat face (inside edge and outside edge). An edge also describes when a ball lightly deflects from the edge of the bat.

extras Runs that are not scored by a batter, i.e. wides, no-balls, byes and leg byes.

feather A faint deflection or edge from the bat.

fifer Five or more wickets taken by a bowler during a single innings.

fishing A batter is fishing when consistently playing at but missing deliveries directed outside the line of off stump.

flash An aggressive swing at a wide delivery.

flat track A pitch with an even surface and a predictable bounce.

four ball A short or wide or a half volley length delivery, all of which are asking to be struck to the boundary.

full toss A delivery that does not bounce before reaching the batter.

gate The gap left between a batter's bat and pad when driving at the ball.

golden duck When a batter is out first ball and with a score of nought.

grubber A delivery that shoots along the ground after bouncing.

half century An individual batter's innings of 50–99 runs.

hat trick When a bowler takes three wickets in three successive deliveries (though not necessarily during a single over).

hole out A lofted shot that is caught near the boundary.

innings The period when a team or individual bats.

jaffa An unplayable delivery that deviates sharply off the pitch.

jagging A delivery deviating sharply from the pitch.

knock The individual innings of a batter.

leg break A leg spin delivery turning from a right-handed batter's leg side towards the off side.

leg bye An extra run scored from a delivery that is deflected by some part of the batter other than the bat or a hand holding the bat.

length The length of a delivery describes how far the ball bounces in front of the batter.

line The line of a delivery describes the direction the ball is travelling in, e.g. an 'off stump line' describes deliveries directed towards off stump.

long hop A short-pitched delivery that sits up and begs to be dispatched to the boundary.

loop The loop describes the trajectory or flight of a delivery.

maiden An over in which no runs are conceded by the bowler. There are no bowling extras (no-balls or wides) but a maiden over may include byes or leg byes.

Nelson A score of 111, considered to be unlucky by some superstitious English cricketers.

nick A ball lightly deflecting from the edge of a bat.

off break An off spin delivery turning from a right-handed batter's off side towards the leg side.

off the mark When a batter scores their first run or runs of their innings.

on side Another name for the leg side of the field of play (the opposite of the off side).

on strike The batter facing the bowling is referred to as on strike.

openers The two batters who bat first for a side.

opening the face Angling the bat face outwards in order to direct the delivery towards the off side.

over An over consists of six fair deliveries.

over pitched A delivery of very full length that should be easy to drive.

over rate The average number of overs bowled per hour.

overthrows Extra runs scored when the ball is not collected at the stumps when returned by a fielder. Overthrows can be caused by a bad bounce, a wild throw, a ricochet from the stumps or by an error committed by the player behind the stumps.

partnership The runs scored by two batters batting together.

pick To detect and successfully predict a variation in the bowler's delivery.

playing on When a batter is bowled out after deflecting the ball from the bat into the stumps.

plumb A straightforward and obvious LBW decision.

rip To 'give the ball a rip', is to impart considerable spin.

rough The areas of the pitch damaged by bowlers' footsteps. Spinners often target the rough areas in order to exaggerate the ball's turn and bounce.

runner A batter who runs between the wickets for an injured team mate.

sitter A simple catch that lobs gently to a fielder.

sledging Verbal abuse of a batter by the fielding side.

slip cordon The collective term for slip fielders.

spell The number of consecutive overs a bowler bowls (e.g. first spell, second spell); or the total number of overs that a bowler bowls during an innings.

square At 90° to the striking batter, i.e. towards the fielding positions of point and square leg; or the square also describes the area in the middle of the playing field encompassing the collection of pitches.

stock delivery A bowler's normal delivery.

strike (striker) The batter receiving a delivery is referred to as the striking batter, having the strike or on strike.

strike bowlers The bowlers in a side that are most likely to take wickets. Strike bowlers are routinely employed to open and close their side's innings.

tail/tail-enders The tail describes the last few batters in a team – usually the side's bowlers.

toe The very bottom edge of a bat.

ton A century; a score of 100 runs or more by one batter in an innings.

the toss Before the game the captains toss a coin for the choice of whether to bat or bowl first.

track Another name for the pitch on which the batter's bat and the bowler's bowl.

turning wicket A pitch particularly receptive to spin bowling.

the V The V shaped region between the fielding positions of mid on and mid off. Hitting in the V suggests batting with a vertically held bat.

walk A batter walks when leaving the field of play without waiting to be given out by an umpire.

wicket A dismissal; or the collective term for the stumps; or a commonly used but not strictly correct term referring to the pitch.

wicket maiden An over during which the bowler takes a wicket, no runs are scored by the batters and there are no bowling extras (no-balls or wides) but a maiden over may include byes or leg byes.

wrong 'un Another term for a googly.

yorker A delivery pitched on or around the popping crease and aimed to slide under the bat. Yorkers can catch the batter unawares and are difficult deliveries to score from.

Taking it further

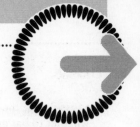

Cricket is played at all levels and by all ages, so if this book has inspired you to progress your cricket then contact a local cricket club who will almost certainly be delighted to accommodate you in an appropriate team. The internet provides the best resource for finding your local cricket club, but you should also be able to find contact details at your library, the local council offices or your regional newspaper.

If you already play competitive cricket you may wish to consider completing a short course and qualifying as a cricket coach or coaching assistant. Courses are run regularly in most regions and completing such a course can significantly improve an individual cricketer's technique and knowledge as well as providing a priceless asset to their cricket club.

Useful websites

▶ Find your local cricket clubs at www.play-cricket.com
▶ Lords – the home of cricket – www.lords.org
▶ The England and Wales Cricket Board is the single national governing body for all cricket in England and Wales – www.ecb.co.uk
▶ The International Cricket Council is the governing body for cricket – icc-cricket.yahoo.net
▶ Cricinfo is the world's leading cricket statistics and cricket news website – www.cricinfo.com.

Index

Image credits